# The
# Ultimate Guide to
# WEIGHT
# TRAINING
## for
# GOLF

*fourth edition*

Prior to beginning any exercise program, you must consult with your physician. You must also consult your physician before increasing the intensity of your training.

Any application of the recommended material in this book is at the sole risk of the reader, and at the readers discretion. Responsibility of any injuries or other negative effects resulting from the application of any of the information provided within this book is expressly disclaimed.

Published by Price World Enterprises
28550 Belcourt Rd
Pepper Pike, OH 44124

Book layout and typesetting by Just Your Type DTP
Cover design by Alexandru Dan Georgescu
Interior photographs by Marc Gollub
Editing by Barb Greenberg
Editing and proofreading by Maryanne Haselow-Dulin
Printing by RJ Communications

Fourth Edition, 2006
ISBN: 1-932549-47-1

Printed in the United States of America
10 9 8 7 6 5 4

Special thanks to:
Dr. Marc B. Price CPFT for your expert insight and helpful contributions
Zack, David, and Gail Price for your support and encouragement to make this book possible.

# The Ultimate Guide to WEIGHT TRAINING for GOLF

*fourth edition*

 *sports*workout.com

# CONTENTS

# Part I

# Golf
# Specific
# Training

# INTRODUCTION

Regardless of its reputation, golf is a physically demanding sport. It requires strength, power, flexibility, balance, muscular endurance, and stamina, each of which can be enhanced through a proper golf-specific weight-training program. This book focuses on how to develop your body in every aspect that is most important to golf. It also provides you with detailed golf-specific programs designed for the off-season, pre-season, and in-season to maximize your golf-playing potential.

Weight training specifically for golf will make your entire body more flexible, fit, and powerful, which, in turn, will give you greater club-head speed and power. It will decrease your vulnerability to injury and increase your muscular endurance. If you train properly for golf you will experience these benefits without sacrificing your technique on the course. Proper weight training can enhance your technique by improving your flexibility and increasing your range of motion. This book not only contains a year-round golf-specific training program, but also includes over 50 additional 4-week programs so you can find exactly what you need.

**Improper Training** Training improperly increases the risk of injury and it can set you further away from your goals. The goal of weight training for golf is not to build stiff, bulky muscles; it is to improve your golf game by increasing your power, flexibility, muscular endurance, and balance. You want to build your muscles and improve flexibility in areas specifically used in your swing, and you want to increase your muscular endurance so that you are able to stay fatigue free on every hole. You do not want to spend time and effort performing exercises that can be detrimental to your game.

**Injury Rehabilitation** Weight training also plays a major role in injury rehabilitation. Muscles that are well trained recover faster from injuries, which will help you avoid chronic pain. With stronger muscles supporting your bones, tendons, and ligaments, you will be less injury prone in all aspects of your life. The most common injury experienced among golfers is pain in the lower back. Lower-back pain makes swinging a club properly very difficult, and is damaging to your game. Strengthening the muscles of the entire mid-section plays a major role in maintaining lower-back health as you age and as you continue to play golf. As you will see, a strong trunk is also one of the major sources of a powerful swing.

**Lower-Back Care** Because the lower back is vulnerable to injury , it is important to take great care of it, both on the course and in the gym. Regardless of your activity, whenever bending over, be sure to keep your back straight. Arching your back places undue stress on your vertebrae and unneeded pain for you. Whether you are picking up your clubs, a dumbbell, or your ball, you must always be sure to bend at the knees and keep your back straight.

**Consistency** In order to improve a skill, you must be consistent. Imagine trying to change your swing every time you play. You would never be able to make serious improvements from one day to the next. Even though weight training and golf are very different activities, carrying some of your techniques to and from the gym will keep consistency in your training. While lifting, be sure to maintain a loose grip on the weights—as if you were holding your club. Do not use a grip that is so loose that you drop the weights; just use a relaxed grip similar to that used during your swing.

## THE SWING

The golf swing can be broken down into many parts and at different angles. Each part of the swing involves a different set of muscles, joints, tendons, and ligaments. Every aspect of swinging the club is equally important to how well you hit the ball. By improving aspects of any one of these areas, you will be improving your swing. By improving all of them, you will experience the benefits to weight training for golf. The programs in this book have you training all of the muscles you use throughout the swing. The most important areas of the body for golf are the hips, mid-section, shoulders, hands, wrists, and hamstrings.

# HIPS

The hips help rotate your body and provide you with explosion and power during the swing. Strong, mobile hips also lead to a more graceful follow through. Exercises in this program that train the hips include lunges and squats.

# MID-SECTION

*Many golfers and strength coaches agree that the mid-section is the most important body part that is used during the swing.*

It is in your mid-section where upper- and lower-body power are transferred. A strong mid-section is also very important in maintaining total body balance. Additionally, a strong mid-section reduces the likelihood of lower-back injury. Later in this book, you will find many helpful techniques on how to maximize your training.

# SHOULDERS

(Scapular muscles and rotator cuffs)

Your swing could not take place without the use of your shoulders and rotator cuffs. The repeated use of your rotator cuffs during the swing places them high on the list of golf-related injuries. The routines provided require a lot of rotator cuff training. Your shoulders supply and transfer power from your mid-section to your arms, which then transfer the power to your hands, and finally to the club. In addition, increased shoulder and upper back flexibility allows for a smoother, easier shoulder turn, giving you greater leverage so you can come down on the ball with greater club-head speed and intensity. An array of different shoulder and upper back exercises are used in each program.

## HANDS AND WRISTS

Hand and wrist strength is also a major element to a powerful golf swing because your hands are the final transfer point of power from your body to the club. Having strong hands and wrists leads to better club control and more controlled shots. Improving your hand and wrist strength for golf is achieved with the use of wrist rollers and hand grippers, and by training your forearms. The best way to attain strong hands and wrists is through the use of wrist rollers because they strengthen both your forearm flexor and extensor muscles through their entire range of motion.

*You can find the most effective wrist rollers on the market for a low price at www.sportsworkout.com*

## HAMSTRINGS

Your entire lower body is used during your swing, but it is your hamstrings that are most important in this area. With more flexibility in your hamstrings, your hips move with greater ease. Flexible hamstrings also help to prevent painful and long-lasting injuries. Strong hamstrings are a major factor in maintaining your balance during and at the end of your swing.

## THE IMPORTANCE OF BALANCE

In golf, good balance cannot be stressed enough. If you are even slightly off balance, your swing will be misplaced and your game will suffer. There are two keys to achieving good body balance.

**Train both sides of the body equally:** It is critical that you train both sides of your body with equal frequency and intensity to achieve good balance. Training one side of the body more often or with greater intensity than the other can lead to one side being heavier than the other, which results in distorted balance as well as possible injuries. To maintain good body balance while weight training, you must train both sides of your body equally.

**Reduce body fat:** Having too much unnecessary weight in the mid-section leads to several problems for golfers. This extra weight in your stomach disrupts your body's balance by causing you to lean forward unintentionally, putting stress on your lower back. As you go through the entire range of motion of the swing, this extra fat-weight disrupts your fluidity. Though it is impossible to reduce fat exclusively from one area of the body, a healthy diet and proper weight training will reduce body fat uniformly throughout your body.

## NEGATIVE EFFECTS OF EXCESSIVE BODY FAT

Aside from damaging your balance, excess fat brings about several other negative effects in golf. Having to carry around extra weight with you on the course wears your muscles down and fatigues your body. You may be walking up to as many as five miles while playing a round of eighteen holes and your body will be wasting the energy you need to stay focused on carrying excess weight as you walk from hole to hole. The resulting muscular and mental fatigue will cause to your game to suffer. The routines provided in this book have been designed on foundations of the most up-to-date fat burning principles to help you achieve your optimum weight.

Sometimes weight training alone is not enough to help you dispose all of your unwanted fat. Therefore, it may be in your best interest to participate in a prolonged low-level aerobic activity such as walking, jogging, or riding the bike to complement your resistance training. Walking while playing is extremely beneficial to your fitness. Taking advantage of this built-in exercise while you are playing is good for your health and will improve your lower-body endurance and strength.

If you are really serious about training for golf you should strongly consider subscribing to our online Sport-Specific e-Training Program where you will be matched up with one of our online sport-specific trainers for one on one training and consultation. Your trainer will create personalized training programs for you based on your specific needs and goals. You will have unlimited access and consultation with your trainer via email 24/7. This program has received fantastic feedback and testimonials from many users and has helped athletes all over the world achieve their goals. To learn more about this program, click the e-Training link on the home page of www.SportsWorkout.com.

## OFF-SEASON TRAINING

The off-season is the time in any sport to build up your muscles, become more powerful, and increase muscular endurance. The off-season program consists of four 4-week routines cycled together to maximize both muscular endurance and explosive power. The first and third routines are designed to build your stamina and muscular endurance, while the second and fourth routines are designed more for power and explosion.

Variation is very important to an effective workout program. Varying your routines keeps you making progress and gains. Your body eventually will adapt to any routine it's on, so it is very important to change routines once your gains have stopped and your strength has peaked. Changing programs every four weeks is the most effective time period to follow any one routine.

**Remember to:**
*After following the fi rst two 4-week off-season programs, be sure to take one week away from the gym to let your muscles rest and grow stronger before beginning your fi nal two 4-week programs.*

During the off-season, you must supplement your weight-training activities with some sort of sport-specific activities to keep your body in proper shape. You must continue to swing the club consistently throughout the off-season to help keep your body loose and ready to play the next season.

## MUSCULAR ENDURANCE TRAINING

The first and third routines of the off-season cycle are to enhance your muscular endurance. Weight training for muscular endurance differs greatly from strength and power training. Strength training builds up size, bulk, and strength; power training builds explosion, speed, and intensity; and endurance training builds your stamina by enabling your muscles to work longer without fatiguing. Weight training to increase your muscular endurance requires many slow movement repetitions to train and build your slow-twitch muscle fibers, which are responsible for increased endurance and stamina.

The keys to endurance training are as follows:

**Low weight, high reps:** Proper endurance training calls for lifting light weights many times. Weights that are less than 60% of your one-rep max are ideal. With more repetitions comes increased muscular endurance, or the ability of your muscles to operate at a high level over time. Every additional repetition helps to increase your muscular endurance. Typically, sets involving at least 20 repetitions are considered to be training your muscular endurance.

**Great form and concentration:** While training for any purpose, great form and concentration are a must. Endurance training is no exception. To get the most of your endurance training, you must breathe properly and perform the exercise with smooth, rhythmic lifts.

**Proper breathing:** As you perform repetition after repetition, your instincts will be to hold your breath. With each and every rep, be sure to inhale while lowering the weight on the eccentric (negative) movement and exhale while raising the weights on the concentric (positive) movement. Never hold your breath.

**Smooth rhythmic lifts:** In endurance training, the lowering, negative part, of every rep should last at least two seconds and the raising, positive part, should be at least one second. The goal is to keep this rhythm from your first rep to your last to ensure a great workout.

**Short rest times:** To get the most out of endurance training, it is best if you take short rest times between sets. This gives lifting aerobic benefits because it leads to a more continuous, less sporadic workout, which keeps your heart rate up. To ensure optimal results while training for endurance, take no more than sixty seconds of rest time between sets.

## EXPLOSIVE-POWER TRAINING

The second and fourth routines of the cycle are designed to build speed and explosive power. The important aspects to explosive power training are as follows:

**Medium weights, medium reps:** Training for power is quite different from training for endurance. For endurance training, the intent is to lift light weights a high number of times. Contrastingly, increasing the weight-load and lifting between eight and fifteen repetitions is the best way to successfully train for power and explosion.

*For power training, you should lift weights that are roughly 70% of your one-rep max.*

**Speed and intensity:** While training for power, the goal is to increase the speed while lifting. Before increasing the load, you want to increase the speed at which you are performing the concentric part, or positive phase, of the lift. If the load begins to feel extremely light, then follow the steps listed in the section *When to Increase* located later in this book for increasing the resistance.

There are certain exercises, however, that should never be performed with speed and intensity due to the possibility of injury, or because fast movements are not as effective as slow ones. Exercises listed in the programs that should never be lifted with speed and intensity are:

1. Lower back exercises
2. Rotator cuff exercises
3. Mid-section exercises

**Great Form:** Similar to endurance training, the lowering of the weight should be smooth and slow for at least two seconds. The difference comes on the concentric part of the lift. For power training you want to raise the weights as fast and explosively as possible, working your fast-twitch muscle fibers with the goal of increasing the speed with which you can contract and move your muscles. While following power-building routines, you are required to perform the concentric part of every rep in every set with intensity and speed. On a very important note, however, you must be sure not to sacrifice form for speed.

Certain exercises are most beneficial and most effectively performed with speed and intensity. Olympic lifts such as push presses and power cleans, as well as body weight exercises like dips and pull-ups, are examples because they can be performed extremely fast with enormous mounts of intensity.

# Golf Off-Season Program

## Endurance and Power Cycle

### Weeks 1-4 Endurance Training

#### Weeks 1-2

Days1 & 3

| muscle group | exercise | sets | reps |
| --- | --- | --- | --- |
| shoulders | barbell military press | 2 | 25,25 |
| shoulders | upright rows | 2 | 25,25 |
| rotator cuff | rotator cuff prone position | 1 | 20 |
| rotator cuff | rotator cuff on side | 1 | 20 |
| legs | lunges | 3 | 20,20,20 |
| legs | squats | 2 | 25,25 |
| triceps | dips | 2 | failure |

Days2 & 4

| muscle group | exercise | sets | reps |
| --- | --- | --- | --- |
| back | seated cable rows | 2 | 25,25 |
| back | behind the neck pull downs | 2 | 25,25 |
| forearms | hammer curls | 2 | 25,25 |
| forearms | behind the back wrist curls | 2 | 30,30 |
| lower back | hyperextensions | 3 | 15,15,15 |
| obliques | side bends | 2 | 20,20 |
| intercostals | intercostal pull overs | 2 | 20,20 |

#### Weeks 3-4

Days1 & 3

| muscle group | exercise | sets | reps |
| --- | --- | --- | --- |
| shoulders | dumbbell military press | 2 | 25,25 |
| shoulders | standing flyes | 2 | 25,25 |
| rotator cuff | rotator cuff prone position | 1 | 20 |
| rotator cuff | rotator cuff on side | 1 | 20 |
| legs | lunges | 3 | 25,25,25 |
| legs | leg press | 2 | 25,25 |
| triceps | close-grip bench press | 2 | 30,30 |

Days2 & 4

| muscle group | exercise | sets | reps |
| --- | --- | --- | --- |
| back | one-arm dumbbell rows | 2 | 25,25 |
| back | behind the neck pull downs | 2 | 25,25 |
| forearms | reverse curls | 2 | 25,25 |
| forearms | reverse wrist curls | 2 | 30,30 |
| lower back | good mornings | 3 | 15,15,15 |
| obliques | oblique crunches | 2 | 20,20 |
| intercostals | intercostal pull overs | 2 | 20,20 |

### Weeks 5-8 Power Training

#### Weeks 5-6

Days1 & 3

| muscle group | exercise | sets | reps |
| --- | --- | --- | --- |
| shoulders | push press | 3 | 12,12,12 |
| shoulders | bent-over lateral raises | 2 | 25,25 |
| rotator cuff | rotator cuff prone position | 1 | 20 |
| rotator cuff | rotator cuff on side | 1 | 20 |
| legs | box steps | 3 | 12,12,12 |
| legs | dead lift | 3 | 12,12,12 |
| triceps | bench dips | 2 | failure |

Days2 & 4

| muscle group | exercise | sets | reps |
| --- | --- | --- | --- |
| back | wide-grip pull-ups | 2 | failure |
| back | bent-over barbell rows | 3 | 12,12,12 |
| forearms | hammer curls | 3 | 12,12,12 |
| forearms | wrist roles | 3 | |
| lower back | hyperextensions | 3 | 15,15,15 |
| obliques | side bends | 2 | 20,20 |
| intercostals | intercostal pull overs | 2 | 20,20 |

#### Weeks 7-8

Days1 & 3

| muscle group | exercise | sets | reps |
| --- | --- | --- | --- |
| shoulders | push press | 3 | 12,12,12 |
| shoulders | front raises | 2 | 25,25 |
| rotator cuff | rotator cuff prone position | 1 | 20 |
| rotator cuff | rotator cuff on side | 1 | 20 |
| legs | box steps | 3 | 12,12,12 |
| legs | lunges | 3 | 12,12,12 |
| triceps | close-grip bench press | 3 | 12,12,12 |

Days2 & 4

| muscle group | exercise | sets | reps |
| --- | --- | --- | --- |
| back | close-grip pull-ups | 2 | failure |
| back | behind the neck pull downs | 2 | 25,25 |
| forearms | reverse curls | 3 | 12,12,12 |
| forearms | wrist roles | 3 | |
| lower back | good mornings | 3 | 15,15,15 |
| obliques | oblique crunches | 2 | 20,20 |
| intercostals | intercostal pull overs | 2 | 20,20 |

## Weeks 9-12 Endurance Training

### Weeks 9-10

Days1 & 3

| muscle group | exercise | sets | reps |
|---|---|---|---|
| shoulders | barbell military press | 2 | 25,25 |
| shoulders | upright rows | 2 | 25,25 |
| rotator cuff | rotator cuff prone position | 1 | 20 |
| rotator cuff | rotator cuff on side | 1 | 20 |
| legs | lunges | 3 | 20,20,20 |
| legs | squats | 2 | 25,25 |
| triceps | dips | 2 | failure |

Days2 & 4

| muscle group | exercise | sets | reps |
|---|---|---|---|
| back | seated cable rows | 2 | 25,25 |
| back | behind the neck pull downs | 2 | 25,25 |
| forearms | hammer curls | 2 | 25,25 |
| forearms | behind the back wrist curls | 2 | 30,30 |
| lower back | hyperextensions | 3 | 15,15,15 |
| obliques | side bends | 2 | 20,20 |
| intercostals | intercostal pull overs | 2 | 20,20 |

### Weeks 11-12

Days1 & 3

| muscle group | exercise | sets | reps |
|---|---|---|---|
| shoulders | dumbbell military press | 2 | 25,25 |
| shoulders | standing flyes | 2 | 25,25 |
| rotator cuff | rotator cuff prone position | 1 | 20 |
| rotator cuff | rotator cuff on side | 1 | 20 |
| legs | lunges | 3 | 25,25,25 |
| legs | leg press | 2 | 25,25 |
| triceps | close-grip bench press | 2 | 30,30 |

Days2 & 4

| muscle group | exercise | sets | reps |
|---|---|---|---|
| back | one-arm dumbbell rows | 2 | 25,25 |
| back | behind the neck pull downs | 2 | 25,25 |
| forearms | reverse curls | 2 | 25,25 |
| forearms | reverse wrist curls | 2 | 30,30 |
| lower back | good mornings | 3 | 15,15,15 |
| obliques | oblique crunches | 2 | 20,20 |
| intercostals | intercostal pull overs | 2 | 20,20 |

## Weeks 13-16 Power Training

### Weeks 13-14

Days1 & 3

| muscle group | exercise | sets | reps |
|---|---|---|---|
| shoulders | push press | 3 | 12,12,12 |
| shoulders | bent-over lateral raises | 2 | 25,25 |
| rotator cuff | rotator cuff prone position | 1 | 20 |
| rotator cuff | rotator cuff on side | 1 | 20 |
| legs | box steps | 3 | 12,12,12 |
| legs | dead lift | 3 | 12,12,12 |
| triceps | bench dips | 2 | failure |

Days2 & 4

| muscle group | exercise | sets | reps |
|---|---|---|---|
| back | wide-grip pull-ups | 2 | failure |
| back | bent-over barbell rows | 3 | 12,12,12 |
| forearms | hammer curls | 3 | 12,12,12 |
| forearms | wrist roles | 3 | |
| lower back | hyperextensions | 3 | 15,15,15 |
| obliques | side bends | 2 | 20,20 |
| intercostals | intercostal pull overs | 2 | 20,20 |

### Weeks 15-16

Days1 & 3

| muscle group | exercise | sets | reps |
|---|---|---|---|
| shoulders | push press | 3 | 12,12,12 |
| shoulders | front raises | 2 | 25,25 |
| rotator cuff | rotator cuff prone position | 1 | 20 |
| rotator cuff | rotator cuff on side | 1 | 20 |
| legs | box steps | 3 | 12,12,12 |
| legs | lunges | 3 | 12,12,12 |
| triceps | close-grip bench press | 3 | 12,12,12 |

Days2 & 4

| muscle group | exercise | sets | reps |
|---|---|---|---|
| back | close-grip pull-ups | 2 | failure |
| back | behind the neck pull downs | 2 | 25,25 |
| forearms | reverse curls | 3 | 12,12,12 |
| forearms | wrist roles | 3 | |
| lower back | good mornings | 3 | 15,15,15 |
| obliques | oblique crunches | 2 | 20,20 |
| intercostals | intercostal pull overs | 2 | 20,20 |

# PRESEASON TRAINING

(Five weeks prior to the start of the season)

When the season begins, you need to be peaking in terms of physical conditioning. The off-season program will have built you up an incredible base of power and endurance. The preseason routine is designed to take you to the next level, making you as powerful as you can become. As you go into the season, your endurance will have increased to the point that even the thought of fatigue will not be an issue.

Every exercise in the preseason program should be performed as a power-building exercise. Lower the weight slowly and smoothly and raise the weight with intensity and bursting explosion. You are required to perform many supersets (performing one set of two exercises, each directly after the other with no rest) in the preseason workout. While performing supersets, you rest after you have completed both sets. Training with supersets is very intense and is helpful for building endurance. See the *Training Techniques* section for more information on supersets.

As the weeks progress, the number of reps required for many exercises decreases and the weight increases, adding a slight aspect of strength training to coincide with the power and endurance training. Power is a product of strength and speed and increasing one of the components will increase your total power. This style of lifting blends all three types of training. The structure of the program is for endurance, your form will be for power, and the increased loads are for strength.

*In the preseason, perform twenty repetitions for all rotator cuff, intercostal, and oblique exercises regardless of the week. Always perform dips until failure regardless of the week.*

# Preseason Training

Purpose: Endurance, Power, and Strength

Style: Holistic Training

Frequency: Two-day split, four days per week

## Reps and Sets

| | |
|---|---|
| Weeks 1 and 2: | 2 sets of 15 reps |
| Weeks 3 and 4: | 3 sets of 12 reps |
| Week 5: | 4 sets of 8 reps |

**Note:** Exercises in bold are exercises that should be supersetted.

### Day 1

| muscle group | exercise |
|---|---|
| shoulders | push press |
| shoulders | **dumbell military press** |
| shoulders | **cable lateral raises** |
| rotator cuff | rotator cuff prone position |
| legs | **squats** |
| legs | **lunges** |
| triceps | triceps kickbacks |

### Day 2

| muscle group | exercise |
|---|---|
| back | **seated cable rows** |
| back | **behind neck pull downs** |
| forearms | **hammer curls** |
| forearms | **wrist curls** |
| lower back | hyperextensions |
| obliques | side bends |
| intercostals | intercostal pull overs |

### Day 3

| muscle group | exercise |
|---|---|
| shoulders | upright rows |
| shoulders | **lateral raises** |
| shoulders | **front raises** |
| rotator cuff | rotator cuff on side |
| legs | **leg press** |
| legs | **box steps** |
| triceps | bench dips |

### Day 4

| muscle group | exercise |
|---|---|
| back | **bent-over dumbbell rows** |
| back | **one-arm dumbbell rows** |
| forearms | **wrist roles** |
| forearms | **reverse wrist curls** |
| lower back | good mornings |
| obliques | oblique crunches |
| intercostals | intercostal pull overs |

# In-Season Training
## Maintenance Training

While in season, the preferred method of training is for maintenance. The goal of inseason weight training is to hang on to the gains you have acquired during the off-season, while being careful not to over train and become stale. When you become stale, your abilities and performance as an athlete decrease drastically. Lifting weights more than twice a week and practicing on a daily basis is more than enough to over train many people.

In order to maintain the endurance and explosion added in the off-season, in-season maintenance training calls for working out your major sport-specific muscle groups two days a week. Training your muscles only once a week can cause them to lose the gains that they have acquired. The in-season routine includes maintenance exercises for endurance, strength, and explosive power elements so that nothing is lost during the season. If you wish, you can perform the in-season routine using a *circuit training format*. For more information on circuit training, see the *Training Techniques* section.

### Odd Weeks
Days 1 & 2

| muscle group | exercise | sets | reps |
|---|---|---|---|
| shoulders | standing flyes | 3 | 15 |
| obliques | oblique crunches | 3 | 15 |
| forearms | wrist roles | 3 | 15 |
| back | one-arm dumbbell rows | 3 | 15 |
| lower back | good mornings | 3 | 15 |
| legs | lunges | 3 | 15 |

### Even Weeks
Days 1 & 2

| muscle group | exercise | sets | reps |
|---|---|---|---|
| shoulders | upright rows | 3 | 15 |
| obliques | side bends | 3 | 15 |
| forearms | behind the back wrist curls | 3 | 15 |
| back | seated cable rows | 3 | 15 |
| lower back | hyperextensions | 3 | 15 |
| legs | squats | 3 | 15 |

*Remember to: -Train your abs prior to each training session*
*- Stretch your muscles directly after each training session*

# PROTEIN: HOW MUCH IS ENOUGH?

*This article was written by Jayson Hunter, RD, CSCS*

Many athletes believe that consuming large amounts of protein will improve their performance. This is true to a certain extent but many still consume way too much protein, which can result in a decrease in performance because other nutrients are then sacrificed. Protein is made up of 21 different amino acids. Once the amino acids are absorbed they are involved in the make up of blood plasma, visceral tissue, and muscle. Amino acids also activate vitamins that are involved in metabolic and physiologic activities. Protein also is responsible for almost 2000 enzymes that help speed up chemical reactions and regulate the breakdown of carbohydrates, fat and proteins that are used for energy.

As you can see protein is a very important nutrient in the body. The only thing is that the body can only use so much at one time and the extra gets stored as carbohydrates or fat. Research is showing that protein requirements of athletes may be determined by their type and amount of physical activity. The current recommended daily allowance for protein is 0.8g/kg of body weight for a normal individual. Many researchers believe that exercise requires a higher protein requirement. They believe that an athletes protein requirements should be in the range of 1.2g/kg - 2.0g/kg depending on their activity. No research has shown that protein intake of greater than 2.0g/kg is more beneficial than the current recommendations for athletes. Total calories are also important for proper utilization of protein. When your body receives enough calories to fuel your activities this allows the protein to solely be utilized for repairing muscle and not used as energy.

An athlete should not eat excess amounts of protein because it may be harmful to their health. An excess intake of protein requires extra water to breakdown the protein, which leads to dehydration and it leads to an increase in urinary calcium loss.

Excess protein may also lead to kidney malfunction but there is limited research in this area.

Most athletes consume plenty of protein so there shouldn't be an urgency to increase your protein intake. An accurate way to determine your protein intake is to keep a 24hr food journal and calculate the amount of protein eaten for the day. Then determine your protein needs by multiplying your body weight in kilograms by 1.2-2.0 grams of protein and see if your daily intake falls into this range. If you are eating more protein than you need then you can decrease the amount because you are not increasing your performance and may be possibly harming your body in the long run.

# Post-Workout Recovery: A must for athletes

*This article was written by Jayson Hunter, RD, CSCS*

If you want to optimize your training, improve recovery time, and accelerate muscle growth then a post-workout recovery drink is vital to your training routine. Research has shown that if you are trying to gain lean body mass you need to feed your body carbohydrates and protein within 60 minutes after your workout.

When you work out your body burns up amino acids, glucose, and glycogen and your muscles are more receptive to accepting the nutrients you feed it and shuttling those nutrients into the muscles to be repaired. When an athlete doesn't restore their fuel levels soon after the workout their muscle glycogen synthesis can be decreased by as much as 66%, which impairs their recovery time. Scientific studies show that consuming a carbohydrate-protein supplement within 60 minutes following exercise increases the rate of muscle glycogen storage. By replacing your glycogen storage levels quickly allows your body to recuperate faster and re-charge your fuel system for the next workout or event. You may also find that you have fuller, tighter muscles as well as less muscle soreness.

A great post-workout supplement should contain around 50-100 grams of carbohydrates and approximately 30-50 grams of protein. Some examples of post-workout drinks could be a Carnation Instant Breakfast with a scoop of protein powder. A glass of orange juice with some protein powder will also work. There are supplement drinks that come pre-mixed and include vitamins, minerals, and sometimes creatine or glutamine. A high carbohydrate/protein meal immediately after your workout is not as effective as a supplement drink, but is excellent for your next meal to further maximize the recovery of your muscles. The reason a meal wouldn't be ideal is that whole foods are digested much slower than liquid meals and can even lower the response of absorbing these nutrients into the blood stream and muscles.

Those first 60 minutes after your workout is when your body's anabolic system is primed for fuel. This will definitely enhance your workouts and your body will thank you with the results you are looking for.

# SPORTS DRINKS AND REHYDRATION: WHAT YOU SHOULD KNOW

*Jayson Hunter, Rd, CSCS*

Sport Drinks are becoming more popular everyday, but do you know when and how you should be drinking them? There are many different types of energy drinks on the market all promoting that their drink is the best.

It isn't which brand you drink, but how you drink it. Energy drinks are beneficial to those that exercise or compete for periods of 60 minutes or longer, or exercise in warmer temperatures. The way that the body absorbs nutrients and fluids is affected by the rate at which they are emptied from the stomach into the small intestine. Some factors that influence gastric (stomach) emptying are that large fluid volumes in the stomach increase the emptying rate into the intestine. Other factors such as increased concentrations of solutes (sugar) and exercise intensity above 75% decreases the gastric emptying rate and may cause stomach upset, and/or diarrhea. An athletes fluid absorption is increased by consuming low to moderate levels of glucose and the temperature of the fluid doesn't seem to play as much of a role in absorption as once thought.

Here are some guidelines to help you choose a proper energy drink. You should avoid drinks that contain high concentrations of particles because it decreases the rate of gastric emptying. There is little difference between liquid glucose, sucrose, or starch when ingested as the carbohydrate fuel source during exercise. Fructose is not a recommended fuel because of its slow absorption and it also promotes low fluid absorption. A re-hydration drink should contain a carbohydrate concentration between 5-8%. Higher concentrations cause a delayed gastric(stomach) emptying and possible stomach upset or diarrhea. To determine the carbohydrate concentration in a drink, divide the carbohydrate content (in grams) by the fluid volume (in milliliters) of the drink and multiply by 100. This range usually allows proper carbohydrate replacement and without limiting fluid absorption, and temperature regulation. Drinks that contain sodium may benefit ultra-endurance athletes by maintaining plasma osmolality, reduces urine output, and sustains the physiological urge to drink.

Consuming 400-600ml of fluid immediately before exercise increases the beneficial effect of having an increased stomach volume, and fluid and nutrient passage into the intestine. You should continue to consume 150-250ml of fluid (at 15 minute intervals) throughout exercise to replenish the fluid that is passed into the intestine and it will also maintain a large gastric volume during exercise. The optimal carbohydrate replacement rate is between 30-60g per hour ingested at least 30 minutes before usual fatigue would have set in without a carbohydrate supplement. Maximal fluid ingestion is about 1000ml per hour to prevent dehydration without gastrointestinal discomfort. Each athlete will have to determine which drink they like best or that will help them perform better. These guidelines should help you maintain proper hydration and optimize performance. The keys to a good energy drink are that it tastes good, offers the potential to improve performance, gets absorbed rapidly and won't cause stomach upset.

# PRE-EVENT FUELING FOR PEAK PERFORMANCE

Jayson Hunter, Rd, CSCS

Some athletes avoid eating before competition because they think it will cause stomach cramps and nausea. Unless you eat immediately before your event this is unlikely to happen. Your performance may suffer though if you don't eat before your game or competition. For those athletes that avoid eating a meal their liver glycogen storage (main source of glucose) can be decreased by as much as 80% depending on whether they compete in the morning or later in the day.

During exercise athletes primarily rely on pre-existing glycogen stores and fat stores. If your pre-event meal is eaten at the proper time then you will be assured that your glycogen stores are plenty full and this will optimize performance. Liquid meals can also be an advantage by digesting more rapidly than solid foods as well as provide hydration. Liquid meals can be eaten closer to competition because they are emptied from the stomach quickly. Pre-event snacks within 1 hour of competition or practice can be more beneficial to athletes that exercise longer than 60 minutes.

It is important to choose primarily carbohydrates before an event because they digest quickly and are readily available for fuel. You can still eat some protein and fat with your meal but high fat meals may leave you feeling sluggish and uncomfortable.

Here are some guidelines for when to fuel prior to your event:

| Hours before event | Meal type | Calories |
|---|---|---|
| 3-5 hours | large meal | 300-500 |
| 2-3 hours | small meal | 200-300 |
| 1-2 hours | liquid meal | 100-200 |
| 0.5-1 hour | snack | 50-100 |

Some examples of meals and snacks are listed below.

| Snacks | Meals |
|---|---|
| Bagel | Baked potato |
| Banana | Breadsticks |
| Cereal Bars | Corn |
| Dried Fruit | Noodles |
| Fig Newtons | Rice |
| Fruit | Baked Beans |
| Graham Crackers | Oatmeal |
| Raisins | Whole Wheat Bread |
| White Bread | Peas |

Both whole foods and liquid meals aid in maintaining optimal muscle glycogen storage and help with maintaining hydration. They also help maintain blood glucose levels during extended exercise bouts. Take advantage of what a properly timed meal can do for your performance.

# Members Only Area

The articles you have just read were taken from Ryan Lee's sport-specific membership.

This member's only resource has over **10,000** pages of sports-training programs, articles, and tips written by many of the world's top authorities on sports fitness training.

*"This Sport-Specific membership is simply the best and most complete sports training resource I've ever used. If you are serious about improving your sports performance **I highly recommend joining today!**"*
**Duane Carlisle**
**NFL** Philadelphia Eagles Speed Consultant

*"I was just introduced to your site by a colleague of mine and I wanted to let you know how impressed I was. **You have a wonderful site... I will certainly recommend that my athletes check out your site.**"*
**Matt Nichol**
**NHL** Toronto Maple Leafs Head Strength Coach

*"The site is an **amazing collection of high-end quality information.** The valued access to the collection of data and articles here far exceeds the membership fee. Great work. Thanks again."*
**Jamie Roche**
**Hebron Academy**, Anatomy & Physiology Teacher, Coach Baseball, Soccer & Hockey

*"This is by far the **most comprehensive site any strength and speed coach could ever want.** Great job Guys!!!"*
**Jude Massillon**
Professional Strength Coach to Several Track/Field Olympians and over 40 NFL 1st Round Draft Choices

**Take a free tour** to see all of the benefits members get by visiting **www.SportsWorkout.com** and clicking the 'Members Only' link.

Get **$5** off and an **extra 6 months free** with Promo Code MEM471

Go to **www.SportsWorkout.com** or call **1-866-SWORKOUT (796-7568)** to Order!

# Part II

# Getting Started

# WARMING UP

Warming up is an essential part of a weight-training routine. *A warm-up activity can be any type of low-level activity as long as it loosens up your body, gets your blood flowing, and prepares your body for the workout.* Warming up is absolutely necessary if you plan to lift heavy weights. To walk into the gym and attempt *to max* out (lift the maximum amount of weight you can handle) without first warming up can cause injury because your body is not ready for the physical stress of a weight-training routine. In general, there are two major types of warming up, which are listed below.

A **full body warm-up** is anything that increases your blood flow and literally warms you up. Examples of full-body warm-up activities include low-intensity activities such as jogging or riding the bike for five to ten minutes prior to lifting weights. Other examples include about five to ten minutes of an abdominal routine, swimming a few laps, or even some full-body stretching.

An **exercise-specific warm-up** is properly executed by performing a light-weight set (group of repetitions) of an exercise before going into your prescribed routine for that same exercise with heavier weights. Ten repetitions are usually enough for a warm-up set. Basing your exercise-specific warm-up set on half of your *one-rep max* is the best technique. Your one-rep max is the maximum weight you can lift one time. Performing an exercise-specific warm-up increases your blood flow to the *active muscles*, that is, the muscles you are using.

**Benefits of Warming Up** One major benefit of warming up is that it helps reduce the likelihood of pulls, tears, and other injuries, which can be painful and hamper your future training. Another major benefit of warming up is that it loosens your muscles and allows you to lift heavier weights. Heavier weights, in turn, put more resistance on your muscles, which forces you work to harder and gives you a better workout.

# COOLING DOWN

Cooling-down activities come directly after your weight-training session. While cooling down, the goal is, again, to loosen up your muscles. In this book, cooldown activities are synonymous with stretching exercises. Cooling-down activities are important because they can prevent soreness in the days following a weight-training session. They also increase your range of motion, helping you become more flexible, which can prevent injuries both in the weight room and in athletics. Because flexibility and range of motion are so important for all sports, stretching is a vital part of a complete workout program and should never be ignored.

There are numerous benefits to stretching and it is most effective during or after your workout. Stretching increases your range of motion and *stretching can be effective in injury reduction.* Proper stretching *may* also be effective in reducing soreness from weight training by helping to remove the anaerobic waste product—lactate—from your muscles.

Range of motion is essential for all sports and physical activities, and stretching is the way to increase it. It is a myth that weight training automatically makes you stiff and decreases your flexibility. Training *antagonistic,* or opposite, muscle groups in the same session actually stretches your muscles and helps increase your range of motion. An example of an antagonistic muscle group is the biceps and triceps. As the biceps contract, the triceps extend, which gives them a nice, full stretch.

# ABS

Having a tight stomach, strong lower back, and incredible six-pack is important for both personal and athletic reasons. The exercises provided in this book will have you training properly and building picture-perfect abs. Lower back and oblique exercises are also incorporated with the abs routine so that your entire torso becomes stronger. Having strong abdominals is essential for high sports performance. With tight abs and a strong lower back, you will be able to run faster and become more explosive. You will also be able to make quicker movements with your torso, which leads to jumping higher and making sharper turns and cuts. Your midsection connects your upper body to your lower body, and it allows you to apply the strength and power collectively in both areas. A stronger midsection will increase your athletic capabilities.

By nature, the muscles in your midsection are different from the other muscles in your body and need to be trained differently in order to achieve maximum results. To train your abs properly, you need the following:

**1. Slow movements:** Abs are made up mostly of slow-twitch muscle fibers, which requires them to be trained with slow movements for optimal results.

**2. Quantity and consistency:** Abdominals need to be trained for muscular endurance, not muscular strength, which requires many, many repetitions that can be performed daily.

**3. Variety:** Your midsection consists of different areas, each of which requires different exercises. To train each area, you need to perform a variety of exercises. Variety with any exercise is an essential part of muscle building and athletic training. Variety allows you to build and tone every part of the muscle you are training.

To keep things simple, this book refers to the areas of the abdomen as the:
- **Upper Abs**
- **Lower Abs**
- **Obliques**

## Preferred Order of Training

Lower abs and oblique exercises are *compound exercises*, that is, they train more than one muscle group at a time. These exercises also train your upper abs. Upper abs exercises, on the other hand, strictly isolate your upper abs. In order to avoid fatigue in the upper abs, which are being worked in every type of abdominal exercise, and could prevent proper lower abs and obliques training, you should train the lower abs first, then the obliques, and lastly the upper abs.

The preferred order of training your abdominals is as follows:
- **Lower Abs**
- **Obliques**
- **Upper Abs**

**Note:** You can train your lower back before or after performing your abdominal exercises, depending on your personal preference.

Training your midsection for at least five minutes prior to lifting is a great way to warm up because you are both warming yourself up by increasing your blood flow, and you are also building and toning your entire midsection. This can be thought of this as killing two birds with one stone. Perform each exercise slowly and smoothly for one full minute without rest. Rest for 30 seconds between exercises.

Listed below are descriptions and pictures demonstrating exactly how to perform each of the recommended midsection exercises. Do not be overwhelmed by the vast number of recommended exercises. You only need to pick four or five of them for each warm-up routine. As your midsection becomes stronger, you should increase the number of exercises you perform so that you continue progressing in strength. Vary your routine constantly by choosing four or five exercises to warm up with one day and a completely new set of four or five exercises the next day.

# ABS EXERCISES

**Definition:** *Prime movers* are the muscles being directly trained in the exercise.

## Standard Sit-ups
### *Prime Movers: Upper abs*

Starting Position:  Lie flat on your back with your knees bent and the soles of your feet flat on the floor. Elevate your tailbone about one inch above the floor. Place your hands on your ears.

Use your abs to lift the upper half of your body as high as you can, hold the position for a second or two, then slowly return to your starting position.

*Tip: By keeping your tailbone elevated, you are working your lower abs, which is a target area for many people.*

## Standard Crunches
### *Prime Movers: Upper abs*

Starting Position:  Lie flat on your back with your feet and knees elevated so that your shins are parallel with the floor.  Elevate your tailbone about one inch above the floor.  Place your hands on your ears.

Use your abs to lift the upper half of your body. Once you've lifted your shoulders about thirty degrees off the floor, hold the position for a second or two, then slowly return to the starting position and repeat.

## Oblique Crunches
### Prime Movers: Obliques

**Starting Position:** Lie on your left side with your legs slightly bent, knees elevated about an inch or two above the floor, and your hands on your ears. Twist your torso to the right and do your best to keep your upper back and shoulders parallel with the floor.

Use your obliques and upper abs to lift your upper body as high as you can and hold for a second or two. Return slowly to the starting position, and repeat. Then perform this exercise lying on your right side.

## Tailbone Lifts
### Prime Movers: Lower abs

**Starting Position:** Lie flat on your back with your feet and knees elevated so that your shins are parallel with the floor and place your hands on your ears.

With your stomach flexed, use your lower abs to raise your tailbone an inch or two off the floor. Hold that position for a second or two before lowering your tailbone back to the floor. Be sure to keep your upper body in the same position throughout the entire range of motion.

## Elbow to Knee Sit-ups
*Prime Movers: Entire torso*

Starting Position: Lie flat on your back with your knees bent and the soles of your feet flat the floor. Place your hands on your ears.

Use your abs to raise your upper body forward while lifting your left foot off the floor so that your knee comes towards your head. Touch your knee to its opposite elbow. Hold that position for a second or two with your abs flexed. Slowly lower yourself back to the starting position and repeat the same movements with your right knee and left elbow.

## Bicycles
*Prime Movers: Entire torso*

Starting Position: Lie flat on your back with your knees bent, legs extended, feet elevated a few inches above the floor, and your hands on your ears.

Use your abs to raise your upper body forward. At the same time, begin to slowly pump

your legs one by one as if you were riding a bicycle. As your knee comes towards to your head, touch your raised knee to its opposite elbow. Hold that position for a second or two with your abs flexed. Go back to the starting point and repeat the same movements with your other knee and elbow.

## Side Bends
### *Prime Movers: Obliques*

Starting Position: Standing upright, hold a dumbbell in your left hand and place your right hand on your head.

Lean your upper body a few inches to the left and use your obliques on the right side of your body to return to the starting position.

## Good Mornings
### *Prime Movers: Lower back*

Starting Position: Stand upright with your feet close together. Rest a barbell behind your neck on your traps. Keep your head tilted back and your back completely straight.

Slowly bend at the waist until you form a ninety-degree angle with your lower body. Slowly return to the starting position and repeat.

## Hyperextensions
### Prime Movers: Lower back

Starting Position: Lie face down on a hyperextension bench. Bend at the waist with your upper body hanging straight down and your hands placed behind your neck. Tilt your head back and keep your back straight.

Slowly raise your upper body until it is parallel with the floor and level with your lower body. Slowly return to the starting position and repeat.

*Tip for hyperextensions and the preceding exercise, good mornings: Do not arch your back at any point because it can result in a painful injury*

## Reach Throughs
### Prime Movers: Upper and lower abs

Starting Position: Lie flat on your back with your legs extended, slightly spread apart, and elevated a few inches above the floor. Extend both your arms behind your head.

Use your abs to lift the upper half of your body up and bring your knees upward so that your shins are parallel with the floor. Simultaneously extend your arms directly in front of you, between your legs. Hold the position for a second or two, slowly return to the starting position, and repeat.

## Leg Raises
*Prime Movers: Lower abs*

*Starting Position:* Lie on the floor with your legs extended and your shoulders and head tilted forward off the floor, putting stress on your upper abs. Place your hands underneath your tailbone to keep it slightly elevated above the floor. Keep your upper body stationary, hands underneath your tailbone, and legs locked throughout the entire range of motion.

Raise your legs off the floor until they form a ninety-degree angle with the floor, allowing your tailbone and lower back to come off the floor in the process. Slowly lower your legs back to the starting position and repeat.

*Tip: To get your legs that high may require a thrust from your abs, which in this case is okay.*


## Intercostal Pull Overs
*Prime Movers: Intercostals*

Starting Position: Lie on a bench with a barbell resting on your chest and your head slightly off the bench. Hold the bar with an overhand grip.

Slowly lift and lower the bar just over and behind your head until you feel a nice stretch in your chest. At this point raise the bar back over your head to the starting position.

*Tip: If having your head partially off of the bench feels awkward and difficult, then perform this exercise with your head resting on the bench.*

# STRETCHING

Stretching is an absolutely crucial part to weight training for sports. It loosens you up, increases your range of motion, and may reduce the chance of injury and soreness in the days following a workout or athletic competition. Stretching is directly related to flexibility. This section goes into depth on how to properly stretch your muscles during or after a workout.

*Everyone knows that stretching increases flexibility, but not everyone knows that lack of stretching decreases flexibility.*

The recommended time for holding each stretch is ten seconds, resting thirty seconds between stretches. While holding a stretch, do not bounce; the stretch is less effective and can cause painful injuries. For every exercise, stretch as far as you can until you feel slight discomfort in the targeted areas. Go no farther once you reach that point. Hold that position for ten seconds as steadily as you can. Proper breathing and technique are extremely important. Do not hold your breath at any time during the stretch. The recommended stretching exercises and their descriptions and pictures are listed on the following pages.

# STRETCHING EXERCISES

## Hamstrings, Legs Crossed
*Muscles stretched: Hamstrings.*

Starting position: Stand upright and cross your left foot over your right, keeping your legs straight. Bending at the waist, reach as far down as you can, and hold. Repeat with other leg.

## Hamstrings, Legs Spread
*Muscles stretched: Hamstrings, groin*

Starting Position: Stand upright and spread your legs slightly wider than shoulder width, keeping them straight.

Bending at the waist, reach as far down as you can to the outside leg and hold. Repeat to the other leg, then reach straight down. Rest between each stretch.

# Hurdler Stretch
*Muscles stretched: Hamstrings, quadriceps.*

Starting Position: Sit on the floor with your right leg extended in front of you and your left leg bent at the knee and pointing behind you.

Bend at the waist and reach as far forward as you can to your right leg and hold.

Repeat with left leg extended.

# Sit and Reach
*Muscles stretched: Hamstrings, lower back.*

Starting Position:  Sit on the floor with both legs extended in front of you.

Reach forward as far as you can towards your feet, and hold.

# Standing Quad Stretch
*Muscles stretched: Quadriceps.*

Starting Position: Stand upright on your left leg.

Grab your right ankle and pull it back as far as you can towards your buttocks and hold.

Repeat with other leg.

## Neck Rolls
*Muscles stretched: Neck.*

Starting Position: Stand upright with your hands on your hips.

Slowly roll your head clockwise in a circular motion using your full range of motion for ten  rotations. Repeat going counterclockwise.


## Across Body Arm Pulls
*Muscles stretched:  Shoulders, upper back*

Starting Position: Stand or sit upright with your back straight. Reach across your body  with your left arm.  Use your right hand to lightly pull and stretch the left arm as far and as close to your body as you can and hold. Repeat with other arm.

## Overhead Arm Pulls

*Muscles stretched: Triceps, shoulders, upper back.*

Starting Position: Stand or sit upright with your back straight.

Reach up and behind your neck with your left arm. Use your right hand to lightly pull and stretch your left arm as far as you can and hold.

Repeat with other arm.

## Butterflies

*Muscles stretched: Groin, hips.*

Starting Position: Sit upright with your back straight and legs tucked in. Touch the soles of your shoes together and hold your toes with your hands. Pull your feet in as close as you can to your body.

With your elbows, lightly push your knees towards the floor as far as you can and hold.

## Seated Back Twists
*Muscles stretched: Lower back, trunk, thighs, and hips.*

Starting Position: Sit upright with your back straight and left leg extended. Bend and cross your right leg over your left. Place your left forearm on the outside of your right leg, your right hand resting palm down on the floor next to you for balance. Twist your body to the right as far as you can and hold. Repeat to the other side.

## Lying Knee Grabs
*Muscles stretched: Glutes, hips.*

Starting Position: Lying flat on your back with your left knee bent and right leg extended, clasp your hands over the upper shin of your left knee.

Gently pull your left leg towards your chest until you feel the stretch and hold.

Repeat with other leg.

## Standing Calves Stretch
*Muscles stretched: Calves.*

Starting Position: Stand leaning forward with your arms in front of you and your hands pushing against a wall. Place your left leg in front of the right.

Bend your left knee while keeping your right heel flat on the floor. Lean as far forward as you can while still keeping your back heel on the floor and hold.

Repeat with other leg.

*Tip: This exercise also can be performed with both feet back.*

# PROPER FORM

## Short- vs. Long-Term Results

In order to make the greatest gains in the least amount of time, you must perform each exercise properly. Lifting weights with bad form is very dangerous and can result in injury. Also, performing an exercise improperly is a waste of time in the gym. Though you may be able to lift heavier weights with improper form, your long-term results would suffer because you would not get as good a workout. You are better off working out for thirty minutes per day with excellent form and technique than lifting for three hours per day with improper form.

There are two movements to lifting a weight: the eccentric (negative) phase and the concentric (positive) phase.

**The eccentric (negative) phase of the lift** is the slow lowering of the weight. During this phase, your muscle is getting longer while still contracting. For example, in the bench press the eccentric phase occurs when you slowly lower the bar to your chest, lengthening your pectorals and triceps. Regardless of your purpose, the eccentric phase of the lift should always be slow and smooth, lasting at least two seconds. Always inhale while performing the eccentric phase of the lift.

*For the best results, the eccentric phase of every lift should last for at least two seconds.*

**The concentric (positive) phase of the lift** is the exertion phase, or actual lifting of the weight. During this phase, the muscle shortens and the muscle cells contract. For example, in the bench press the concentric phase occurs when you lift the bar up from your chest so that your pectorals and triceps contract. The concentric phase of every lift should last at least one second unless you are training for power and explosion, where you lift the weight concentrically as fast as you can. Always exhale while performing the concentric phase of the lift.

## PROPER BREATHING

**DO NOT HOLD YOUR BREATH while lifting!** Holding your breath can build up pressure in your body. Although extremely rare, if the pressure becomes extraordinarily intense, it can cut off blood circulation to your heart and brain. To avoid problems, just remember to breathe. Remember, you will get the most out of your lifting by inhaling on the eccentric part of the lift and exhaling while performing the concentric part of the lift.

**INHALE** on the eccentric part of every lift,

**and**

**EXHALE** on the concentric pat of every lift.

**Important note:** If you have the determination to get to the gym for a set amount of time, then train with proper form and intensity so that you spend your time efficiently. Many people come home from the gym and feel a false sense of achievement simply because they had "made it to the gym." Once there, you need to work hard so you can *honestly* feel good about yourself for having taken one step closer to achieving your goals. Rather than going back to the gym over and over again to try and make up for lost time, do it right the first time.

# Part III

# Recommended

# Exercises

This section provides you with every recommended weight-training exercise. You are given complete descriptions and pictures to ensure that you perform the exercises properly, safely, and effectively.

The numbers next to the exercises refer to their order of interchangeability, which is discussed in the following subsection. The muscles listed first after "prime movers" are the muscles that are being directly trained. Along with the descriptions are many helpful tips.

## Substituting Similar Exercises

Our weight-training specialists did the hard work for you by strategically designing each program; all you have to do is follow them. Sometimes, however, there may be a required exercise or two that you either cannot perform physically or for which you do not have the equipment to perform. Many people struggle to do certain body weight exercises such as pull-ups or dips. Others may not have access to certain weight-training equipment such as cable or leg press machines. For these reasons, the exercises are listed for you are in order of interchangeability. If there is an exercise in your routine that you are not able to perform, substitute an exercise with a corresponding number from the same section. This substitution will ensure that you are training the same muscle groups in a similarly effective manner.

# CHEST EXERCISES

## Interchangeable Chest Exercises

1 Barbell Bench Press

1 Dumbbell Bench Press

1 Pushups

2 Incline Barbell Bench Press

2 Incline Dumbbell Bench Press

3 Flyes

3 Incline Flyes

3 Cable Crossovers

Dips (can be interchanged with any chest, shoulder, or triceps exercise)

## SAFETY TIP!

*When using a cable machine do not lower the weights so low or fast that they hit the weight stack. This stops the fluid motion of the lift and can cause injuries.*

## Barbell Bench Press
*Prime movers: Chest, triceps, shoulders.*

Starting Position: Lie on a flat bench with your feet flat on the floor. Keep your eyes directly below the bar and your hands shoulder width apart. Lift the bar off its supports until your arms are extended.

Lift:

a. Slowly lower the bar until it grazes you chest. The bar should come to a brief, complete stop.

b. Push the bar back to full extension with the bar directly in line with your chin.

> *Tip: Do not arch your back to try and lift more weight because it can cause serious back problems.*

> *Tip: A closer grip trains your inner chest and triceps well; a wider grip works your outer chest.*

## Dumbbell Bench Press
*Prime movers: Chest, triceps, shoulders.*

Starting Position: Lie on a flat bench with your feet flat on the floor. Hold the dumbbells with your arms extended.

Lift:

a. Slowly lower the dumbbells until you feel a comfortable stretch in your chest. The dumbbells should come to a brief, complete stop slightly below your chest.

b. Push the dumbbells back to full extension.

> *Tip: Dumbbells allow you to bring the weight lower than barbells, training your chest over the entire range of motion in ways a barbell cannot.*

## Pushups
*Prime movers: Chest, shoulders, triceps.*

Starting Position: Lie face down on the floor with your back straight and palms on the floor, shoulder width apart, your legs locked, and your toes on the floor with your heels in the air.

Lift:

**a.** Push your body upward off of the floor until your arms are fully extended.

**b.** Slowly lower yourself until your chest is about an inch from the floor with your legs remaining locked. Come to a brief, complete stop before continuing.

*Tip: To really train your triceps well, put your hands together and form a triangle with your index fingers and thumbs.*

## Incline Barbell Bench Press
*Prime movers: Upper chest, triceps, shoulders.*

Starting Position: Lie on an inclined bench with your feet flat on the floor. Keep your eyes directly below the bar and your hands shoulder width apart.

Lift: Lift the bar off of its supports until your arms are extended.

**a.** Slowly lower the bar until it grazes your chest. The bar should come to a brief, complete stop.

**b.** Push the bar back to full extension with the bar directly in line with your chin.

*Tip: You will not be able to lift as much as with a regular bench press. The steeper the degree of an incline, the less weight one typically is able to lift.*

## Incline Dumbbell Bench Press

*Prime movers: Upper chest, triceps, shoulders.*

Starting Position: Lie on an inclined bench with your feet flat on the floor. Hold the dumbbells with your arms extended in the starting position.

Lift:

a. Slowly lower the dumbbells until you feel a comfortable stretch in your chest. The dumbbells should come to a brief, complete stop slightly below your chest.

b. Push the dumbbells back to full extension.

## Flyes

*Prime movers: Chest.*

Starting Position: Lie on a bench with your feet flat on the floor. Hold the dumbbells with your arms extended and your palms facing each other so that the dumbbells are touching.

Lift:

a. Slowly lower the dumbbells away from each other with your arms slightly bent. Extend the dumbbells as wide as you can until you feel a comfortable stretch in your chest.

b. The dumbbells should come to a brief, complete stop slightly below your chest with your palms facing upward. Use your chest muscles to bring the dumbbells back to the starting position the same way they were brought down.

*Tip: As you bring the dumbbells together, rotating your wrists and touching the tops and bottoms of the dumbbells together is a nice change of pace and trains your muscles from different angles.*

## Incline Flyes
### Prime movers: Chest.

Starting Position: Lie on an inclined bench with your feet flat on the floor. Hold the dumbbells with your arms extended and your palms facing each other so that the dumbbells are touching.

Lift:

a. Slowly lower the dumbbells away from each other with your arms slightly bent. Extend the dumbbells as wide as you can until you feel a comfortable stretch in your chest.

b. The dumbbells should come to a brief, complete stop slightly below your chest with your palms facing upward. Use your chest muscles to bring the dumbbells back to the starting position the same way they were brought down.

## Cable Crossovers
### Prime movers: Chest.

Starting Position: Stand bent slightly forward with your back straight and, with cables on both sides and slightly behind you, grab hold of the cables.

Lift:

a. With your arms slightly bent, use your chest to slowly bring the cables towards each other where they will pass each other in front of you. Cross the cables as far as you can.

b. The cables should come to a brief, complete stop. Then, slowly allow the cables to go back to the starting position the same way they were brought across.

*Tip: Alternate which arm is on top and bottom for every rep to ensure both sides are getting equal training.*

## Dips

*Prime movers:  Chest, shoulders, triceps.*

Starting Position: With arms extended, grip the parallel bars with both hands so that your body is elevated off the floor.

Lift:

a. With your elbows tucked in as closely as possible and your back straight, slowly lower yourself until your chin is parallel with the bars.

b.  Use your chest muscles, shoulders, and triceps to push back up to full extension with your arms locked.

> *Tip: The farther you lean your body forward, the more your chest gets trained.  As you straighten your body, your triceps begin to do the bulk of the work.*

# BACK (LATS) EXERCISES

## Interchangeable Back (Lats) Exercises

> 1 Lat Pull Downs
>
> 1 Behind-the-Neck Pull Downs
>
> 1 Seated Cable Rows
>
> 1 Pull-ups
>
> 2 Bent-Over Barbell Rows
>
> 2 Bent-Over Dumbbell Rows
>
> 2 T-bar Rows
>
> 2 One-Arm Dumbbell Rows

## Lat Pull Downs
*Prime movers: Lats, biceps, shoulders.*

Starting Position: Sit at a lat pull down machine. Keep your back straight and lean backward a few inches with your feet resting on the floor. Grab the bar with both hands, using an overhand grip.

Lift:

a. Keeping your body stationary and bending at the elbows, pull the bar down in front of your neck, squeezing your shoulder blades together until the bar grazes your chest.

b. Let the bar come to a brief, complete stop before slowly and controllably guiding it back up to its original starting position, the same way you pulled it down.

*Tip: This exercise can also be performed with an underhand grip.*

*Tip for all pull downs and pull-ups: The wider the grip, the more you train the upper part of your back. The closer the grip, the more you train the lower part of the back.*

## Behind-the-Neck Pull Downs:
### *Prime movers: Lats, shoulders, biceps.*

Starting Position: Sit upright at a lat pull down machine. Keep your back straight with your feet resting on the floor. Grab the bar with both hands, using an overhand grip.

Lift:

a. Keeping your body stationary and bending at the elbows, pull the bar down behind your neck, squeeze your shoulder blades together, and bring the bar as low as you can.

b. Let the bar come to a brief, complete stop before slowly and controllably guiding it back up to its original starting position, the same way you pulled it down.

*Tip: More flexible people will be able to pull the bar down lower. Do not pull the bar down so low that it starts to feel uncomfortable. If you feel any unusually pain, DO NOT perform this exercise.*

## Seated Cable Rows
### Prime movers: Lats, biceps, shoulders.

Starting Position: Sit at a row machine with your back straight, feet resting on the foot rests and legs slightly bent. Lean forward and grab the handles.

Lift:

a. Keeping your back straight, lean backward and pull the handles towards your stomach as far back as you can, squeezing your shoulder blades together.

b. Let the handles come to a brief, complete stop before slowly and controllably guiding them back up to their original starting position, the same way you pulled them up.

## Pull-ups
### Prime movers: Lats, biceps, shoulders

Starting Position: Grab hold of a pull-up bar using an overhand grip with your arms completely extended and feet crossed and off the floor.

Lift:

a. Keeping your body stationary, feet crossed, and bending at the elbows, pull your body up in front of the bar as high as you can, squeezing your shoulder blades together.

b. Let your body come to a brief, complete stop before slowly and controllably lowering it back up to its original starting position, the same way you pulled it up.

*Tip: This exercise can also be performed behind the neck or with an underhand grip.*

*Tip: To train for optimal results, be sure to lower yourself all the way until your arms are nearly extended.*

## Bent-Over Barbell Rows
*Prime movers: Lats, biceps, shoulders.*

Starting Position: Standing with your knees slightly bent, feet a couple of inches apart, and bending at the waist to form an approximate ninety-degree angle, hold a bar with your arms hanging in front of you. Keep your back straight and your head tilted back.

Lift:

a. Keeping your body stationary and bending at the elbows, pull the bar up towards your stomach squeezing your shoulder blades together.

b. Let the bar come to a brief, complete stop before slowly and controllably guiding it back up to its original starting position, the same way you pulled it up.

Tip for all bent-over back exercises: Do not pull the weights towards your chest; this does not isolate your lats as well as raising the bar to your stomach.

## Bent-Over Dumbbell Rows
*Prime movers: Lats, biceps, shoulders.*

Starting Position: Standing with your knees slightly bent, feet a couple of inches apart, and bending at the waist to form an approximate ninety-degree angle, hang your arms to the sides and hold two dumbbells with your palms facing each other. Keep your

back straight and your head tilted back.

Lift:

a. Keeping your body stationary and bending at the elbows, pull the dumbbells up the sides of your body as high as you can, squeezing your shoulder blades together.

b. Let the dumbbells come to a brief, complete stop before slowly and controllably guiding them back up to their original starting position, the same way you pulled them up.

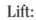

# T-bar Rows
## Prime movers: Lats, biceps, shoulders.

Starting Position: Standing with your knees slightly bent, feet a couple of inches apart, and bending at the waist to form a forty-five-degree angle with your floor, use an overhand grip to hold the handles of a T-bar machine, keeping the weights off of the floor. Keep your back straight and your head tilted back.

Lift:

a. Keeping your body stationary and bending at the elbows, pull the bar up towards your chest squeezing your shoulder blades together.

b. Let the bar come to a brief, complete stop before slowly and controllably guiding it back up to its original starting position, the same way you pulled it up.

*Tip: If no T-bar machines are available, you can make your own using a barbell and a cable bar, as shown in the picture.*

# One-Arm Dumbbell Rows

*Prime movers: Lats, biceps, shoulders*

Starting Position: Standing with your left hand and left knee resting on a bench, bend at the waist to form an approximate ninety-degree angle. Hang your right arm to the side and hold the dumbbell with your palm facing towards your body. Keep your back straight and your head tilted back.

Lift:

a. Keeping your body stationary and bending at the elbow, pull the dumbbell up the side of your body as high as you can.

b. Let the dumbbell come to a brief, complete stop before slowly and controllably guiding it back up to its original starting position, the same way you pulled it up.

# SHOULDERS EXERCISES

## Interchangeable Shoulder Exercises

1 Barbell Military (Shoulder) Press

1 Dumbbell Military (Shoulder) Press

1 Push Press (Jerks)

2 Front Raises

2 Lateral Raises

2 Bent-Over Lateral Raises

2 Cable Lateral Raises

3 Standing Flyes

3 Upright Rows

4 Barbell Shrugs

4 Dumbbell Shrugs

5 Rotator Cuff Prone Position

5 Rotator Cuff On Side

## Barbell Military (Shoulder) Press
*Prime movers: Shoulders, triceps.*

Starting Position: Stand or sit upright and hold a bar at your shoulders, using an overhand grip. Grip the bar with your hands slightly wider than shoulder width.

Lift:

a. Keeping your body still, push the bar straight up until your arms are extended.

b. Slowly lower the bar down to the original starting position.

## Dumbbell Military (Shoulder) Press
*Prime movers: Shoulders, triceps.*

Starting Position: Stand or sit upright and hold dumbbells at your shoulders. Hold them with your hands slightly wider than shoulder width.

Lift:

a. Keeping your body still, push the dumbbells straight up until your arms are extended.

b. Slowly lower the dumbbells down to their original starting position.

## Push Press (Jerks)
*Prime movers: Shoulders, triceps, legs.*

Starting Position: Stand with your back straight and knees slightly bent. Hold the bar at your shoulders using an overhand grip. Grip the bar with your hands slightly wider than shoulder width.

a. Explode upwards with your legs to give the bar some upward momentum. With this momentum, push the bar straight up until your arms are extended.

b. Slowly lower the bar down and return to the starting position.

# Front Raises
*Prime movers: Shoulders, traps.*

**Starting Position:** Stand or sit upright and hold two dumbbells in front of you with your palms facing towards your body.

**Lift:**

**a.** With your arms remaining straight, raise the dumbbells out in front of you in one smooth, fluid motion until your hands are slightly above your shoulders.

**b.** Let the dumbbells come to a brief, complete stop before slowly lowering them back down to their original starting position, the same way you raised them up.

## Tip for All Shoulder Raises

*Once you raise your arms beyond a ninety-degree angle with your body, you begin to focus more on your traps.*

## Lateral Raises
### *Prime movers: Shoulders, traps*

Starting Position: Stand or sit upright and hold two dumbbells at your sides with your palms facing your body.

Lift:

a. With your arms remaining straight, raise the dumbbells out to your sides in one smooth, fluid motion until your hands are slightly above your shoulders and slightly in front of you. As they reach this position, rotate your thumbs downward as if you are pouring a glass of water.

b. Let the dumbbells come to a brief, complete stop before slowly lowering them back down to their original starting position, the same way you raised them up.

*Tip: This exercise can also be performed with your palms pointing upward towards the ceiling.*

*Tip for all shoulder raises: You can raise the dumbbells with both arms at the same time or alternate arms.*

## Bent-Over Lateral Raises
### Prime movers: Shoulders, traps.

Starting Position: Stand or sit bent at the waist, keeping your back completely straight and forming a ninety-degree angle with your legs. Let your arms hang straight down in front of you with your palms facing each other.

**Lift:**

a. With your arms remaining straight, raise your arms out to your sides until they are parallel with your shoulders and slightly in front of you. As they reach shoulder level, rotate your thumbs downward in one smooth, fluid motion as if you are pouring a glass of water.

b. Let the dumbbells come to a brief, complete stop before slowly lowering them back down to their original starting position the same way you raised them up.

## Cable Lateral Raises

### Prime movers: Shoulders, traps.

Starting Position: Stand with your right arm next to a cable machine with your back straight. Grab hold of the cable with your left arm, so that your arm is hanging, slightly bent, across the front of your body. Rest the hand you are not using on your hip.

**Lift:**

a. Keeping your body still and your arm slightly bent, raise the cable across your body and out to the side in one motion until your hand is elevated slightly above your shoulder. As it reaches this level, rotate your thumbs downward in one smooth, fluid motion as if you are pouring a glass of water.

**b.** Let the cable come to a brief, complete stop before slowly lowering it back down to its original starting position the same way you raised it up.

## Standing Flyes
*Prime movers: Shoulders, traps.*

Starting Position: Stand upright or with your knees slightly bent and bend at the waist with your back straight to form a forty-five-degree angle with your lower body. With your palms facing each other, hold two dumbbells a few inches in front of your chest with your elbows bent at ninety-degree angles.

Lift:

**a.** Keeping your body still and your arms bent at 90-degree angles, pull the weights upward and backward as far back as you can, squeezing your shoulder blades together.

**b.** Come to a brief, complete stop before slowly returning the weights back to their starting position the same way you raised them up.

*Tip for standing flyes and upright rows: Avoid using your back and body momentum to complete these lifts because doing so is not an effective way of training and could cause injury.*

## Upright Rows
*Prime movers: Shoulders, traps, biceps.*

Starting Position: Stand upright with your arms hanging in front of you. Hold a barbell with an overhand grip. Your hands should be roughly eight inches apart.

Lift:

a. Keeping your body still and back straight, raise the bar upwards to your chin, keeping the bar as close to your body as you can without touching it.

b. Let the bar come to a brief, complete stop before slowly lowering it back down to its original starting position the same way you raised it up.

## Barbell Shrugs
*Prime movers: Traps*

Starting Position: Stand upright with your arms hanging in front of you. Hold a barbell with an overhand grip, hands roughly shoulder-width apart.

Lift:

a. Keeping your body still, back straight, and arms hanging in front of you, raise only your shoulders straight up.

b. Hold the position for at least three seconds before slowly lowering your shoulders back down to the original starting position.

## Dumbbell Shrugs
### *Prime movers: Traps*

Starting Position: Stand upright with arms hanging at your sides. Hold dumbbells with your palms facing each other.

Lift:

a. Keeping your body still, back straight, and arms hanging at your sides, raise only your shoulders straight up.

b. Hold the position for at least three seconds before slowly lowering your shoulders back down to the original starting position.

## Rotator Cuff Prone Position

*Area trained: Rotator cuff.*

Starting Position: Lie face down on a bench with one arm extended to the side so that your upper arm is parallel to the floor. Bend your arm at a ninety-degree angle so that your hand is hanging with your palm facing behind you. Hold a light weight in that hand.

Lift:

a. Keeping everything else stationary, rotate your forearm upward until it becomes parallel with the ground.

b. Slowly lower the weight back to its original starting position, the same way you brought it up.

*Tip: All rotator cuff exercises should always be performed very slowly and smoothly, and the weights for these exercises should NEVER exceed three lbs. or injuries will occur.*

## Rotator Cuff on Side

*Area trained: Rotator cuff.*

Starting Position: Lie on your side on a bench with your upper arm resting on your chest, parallel to the floor, and bent at the elbow at a ninety-degree angle so that your hand is hanging. Hold a light weight in that hand.

Lift:

a. Keeping everything else stationary, rotate your arm upward until it becomes parallel with the ground.

b. Slowly lower the weight back to its original starting position, the same way you brought it up.

# TRICEPS EXERCISES

## Interchangeable Triceps Exercises

1 Triceps Push Downs

1 Triceps Pull Downs

1 Skull Crushers

1 Triceps Kickbacks

1 Bench Dips

2 Barbell Triceps Curls

2 Dumbbell Triceps Curls

2 One-Arm Triceps Extensions

## Triceps Push Downs
**Prime movers: Triceps.**

Starting Position: Stand or kneel with your back straight in front of a cable machine. Grab the bar with an overhand grip. Keep your elbows tucked in at your sides and hold the bar up by your chin.

Lift:

a. Keeping your body still and elbows tucked at your sides, push the bar straight down until your arms are fully extended.

b. Come to a brief, complete stop before slowly allowing the bar to rise back up to the starting position, with your elbows remaining tucked at your sides at all time.

*Tip: For variation, you can use many types of bars, including one-arm handles.*

## Triceps Pull Downs

*This exercise is identical to triceps push downs with an underhand grip.*

## Skull Crushers
*Prime movers: Triceps.*

Starting Position: Lie on a bench with your head partially hanging off the end. Hold a barbell with a close overhand grip straight out in front of you, above your forehead, with your arms extended.

Lift:

a. Keeping your body still and elbows motionless, slowly lower your forearms and the barbell down behind your head as far as you can.

b. Come to a brief, complete stop before returning the barbell to the starting position the same way you brought it down. Keep your elbows in and do not use your shoulders.

*Tip: If having your head partially off of the bench feels awkward and difficult, then perform this exercise with your head resting on the bench.*

*If balance becomes an issue while performing any cable machine triceps exercise, stand stagger stepped, with one leg behind the other.*

## Triceps Kickbacks
*Prime movers: Triceps.*

Starting Position: Stand bending at the waist so your upper body is parallel with the floor with your knees slightly bent. Stand stagger stepped or place one knee on a bench and place your opposite hand on a bench for balance. With your elbow tucked in at your side and your upper arm also parallel to the floor, let your lower arm hang down perpendicular to the floor.

Lift:

a. Keeping your body still and elbow motionless, raise your lower arm backward until your arm is fully extended.

b. Come to a brief, complete stop before slowly lowering the dumbbell to the starting position, the same way you brought it up. Keep your elbow in and do not use your shoulder.

## Bench Dips
*Prime movers: Triceps, shoulders.*

Starting Position: Place your heels on one bench in front of you and your palms on another bench behind you shoulder-width, leaving your rear hanging in the air. Your heels should be together and your hands should be shoulder-width apart. Your arms should be extended so that your body is elevated.

Lift:

a. Slowly lower yourself by bending at the elbows as low as you can by keeping the elbows tucked in as much as possible and keeping your back straight.

b. Push yourself back up to full extension with your arms locked.

*Tip: If your body weight alone is not providing enough resistance for a good workout, try placing some weights on your lap.*

## Barbell Triceps Curls
*Prime movers: Triceps.*

Starting Position: Stand or sit upright and hold a barbell above your head with your arms locked out and your elbows close to your head.

Lift:

a. Keeping your body still and elbows fixed close to your head, slowly lower your forearms and the bar down behind your head as far as you can.

b.  Come to a brief, complete stop before returning the bar to the starting position, the same way you brought it down.  Keep your elbows in and do not use your shoulders.

> *Tip: Keeping your elbows in close to your head is sometimes difficult to do, but it ensures the best triceps workout.*

## Dumbbell Triceps Curls
*Prime movers: Triceps.*

Starting Position: Stand or sit upright and hold a dumbbell above your head with both hands, your arms locked out, and your elbows close to your head.

Lift:

a. Keeping your body still and elbows fixed close to your head,  slowly lower your forearms and the dumbbell down as far as you can.

b. Come to a brief, complete stop before returning the dumbbell to the starting position, the same way you brought it down.  Keep your elbows in and do not use your shoulders.

# One-Arm Triceps Extensions
*Prime movers: Triceps.*

Starting Position: Stand or sit upright and hold a dumbbell above your head with one hand.  Keep your arm locked out and your elbow close to your head.

Lift:

a. Keeping your body still and elbow fixed close to your head, slowly lower your forearm and the dumbbell down behind your head as far as you can.

b.   Come to a brief, complete stop before returning the dumbbell to the starting position, the same way you brought it down.  Keep your elbow in and do not use your shoulder.

# BICEPS/FOREARMS EXERCISES

## Interchangeable Biceps/ Forearms Exercises

1 Barbell Curls

1 Dumbbell Curls

1 Preacher Curls

1 Incline Dumbbell Curls

1 Concentration Curls

2 Reverse Barbell Curls

2 Reverse Dumbbell Curls

2 Hammer Curls

3 Behind Back Wrist Curls

3 Reverse Wrist Curls

## Barbell Curls
*Prime movers: Biceps.*

Starting Position: Stand upright with your feet roughly shoulder-width apart. Hold a barbell with your palms facing away from your body and elbows tucked into your sides.

Lift:

a. Keeping your elbows tucked at your sides at all times, use your biceps to curl the bar upward as high as you can until it is just below your chin.

b. With your elbows still tucked at your sides, slowly lower the bar back to its original starting position.

> *Tip: Performing cheat curls (allowing your body to rock backward slightly to gain momentum) with this exercise from time to time can be beneficial to gaining mass in the biceps. You MUST wear a weight-lifting belt if you perform cheat curls.*

## Dumbbell Curls
*Prime movers: Biceps.*

**Starting Position:** Stand or sit upright and with your feet roughly shoulder-width apart, hold dumbbells with your palms facing away from your body and elbows tucked into your sides.

Lift:

**a.** Keeping your elbows tucked at your sides at all times, use your biceps to curl the dumbbells upward as high as you can. You can curl with both arms at the same time or alternate arms.

**b.** With your elbows still tucked at your sides, slowly lower the bar back to its original starting position.

**Tip for all dumbbell biceps exercises:**
*Rotating your wrists inward towards your body will add extra emphasis and will give your biceps an even greater peak.*

## Preacher Curls
*Prime movers: Biceps.*

Starting Position: Sit at a preacher bench with your elbows resting on the bench shoulder-width apart. Grip the bar with your palms facing upward.

Lift:

a. With your elbows remaining stationary, use your biceps to curl the bar upward as high as you can towards your chin, where you should flex your biceps for extra emphasis.

b. Slowly lower the bar back to its original starting point with your arms fully extended.

*Tip: A closer grip trains your outer biceps and a wider grip trains your inner biceps.*

## Incline Dumbbell Curls
*Prime movers: Biceps.*

Starting Position: Sit on an inclined bench with your elbows tucked at your sides and your arms fully extended. Grip the dumbbells with your palms facing upward.

Lift:

a. Keeping your elbows tucked at your sides at all times, use your biceps to curl the dumbbells upward as high as you can. You can curl with both arms at the same time or alternate arms.

b. With your elbows still tucked at your sides, slowly lower the bar back to its original starting position.

## Concentration Curls
*Prime movers: Biceps.*

Starting Position: Sit on a bench slightly bent forward with your left arm gripping a dumbbell hanging between your legs. Your left palm should face your right leg and your right arm should rest on your knee.

Lift:

a. Keeping your elbow and upper arm stationary, curl the weight upward towards your shoulder.

b. With your elbow and upper arm still stationary, slowly lower the bar back to its original starting position.

## Reverse Barbell Curls
*Prime movers: Forearms, biceps.*

Starting Position: Stand upright with your feet roughly shoulder-width apart. Hold a barbell with your palms towards your body, your wrists locked, and elbows tucked into your sides.

Lift:

a. Keeping your elbows tucked at your sides and wrists locked at all times, use your forearms and biceps to curl the bar upward as high as you can or until it is just below your chin.

b. With your elbows still tucked at your sides, slowly lower the bar back to its original starting position.

*Tip: Keeping your wrists locked adds extra emphasis to your forearms and ensures a great workout.*

## Reverse Dumbbell Curls
### Prime movers: Forearms, biceps.

Starting Position: Stand or sit upright with your feet roughly shoulder-width apart. Hold two dumbbells with your palms facing towards your body, your wrists locked, and elbows tucked into your sides.

Lift:

a. Keeping your elbows tucked at your sides and wrists locked at all times, use your forearms and biceps to curl the dumbbells upward as high as you can. You can curl with both arms at the same time or alternate arms.

b. With your elbows still tucked at your sides and wrists locked, slowly lower the bar back to its original starting position.

## Hammer Curls
### Prime movers: Forearms, biceps.

Starting Position: Stand or sit upright with your feet roughly shoulder-width apart. Hold two dumbbells with your palms facing each other, your wrists locked, and elbows tucked into your sides.

Lift:

a. Keeping your elbows tucked at your sides, wrists locked, and palms facing each other at all times, use your forearms and biceps to curl the dumbbells upward as high as you can. You can curl with both arms at the same time or alternate arms.

b. With your elbows still tucked at your sides, wrists locked, and palms facing each other, slowly lower the dumbbells back to their original starting position.

## Behind Back Wrist Curls
*Prime movers: Forearms.*

Starting Position: Stand upright with your feet roughly shoulder-width apart. Hold a barbell behind your back as if you are handcuffed with your palms facing away from your body and elbows tucked into your sides.

Lift:

a. Keeping your elbows tucked at your sides at all times, use your wrists to curl the bar upward towards your forearms.

b. With your elbows still tucked at your sides, slowly lower the bar with your wrists back to its original starting position.

## Reverse Wrist Curls
*Prime movers: Forearms.*

Starting Position: Sit at the end of a bench. Hold a barbell with an overhand grip with your palms facing the floor and your forearms resting on your thighs.

Lift:

a. Keeping everything stationary, use your wrists to curl the bar backwards as far as you can.

b. Slowly lower the bar with your wrists, back to its original starting position.

# LEGS EXERCISES

## Interchangeable Leg Exercises

**1 Squats**

**1 Leg Press**

**1 Dead Lift**

**1 Leg Extensions**

**1 Leg Curls**

**2 Standing Calf Raises**

**2 Seated Calf Raises**

**2 Reverse Calf Raises**

**3 Jump Squats**

**3 Power Cleans**

**4 Box Steps**

**4 Lunges**

## Squats
*Prime movers: Upper and lower legs.*

Starting Position: Stand upright with your feet shoulder-width apart and a barbell resting behind your neck on your traps with your hands slightly wider than shoulder-width apart, using an overhand grip. Keep your back straight and your head tilted up.

Lift:

a. With your back remaining straight and your head tilted up, slowly lower the weight by bending your knees until the upper part of your legs is parallel with the floor.

b. Explode upward back to the starting position. The entire lift should be in one smooth, fluid motion.

*Tip for squats and dead lifts: Standing up on your toes as high as you can and holding it for a second or so upon returning to the starting position is a great built-in calves workout.*

## Leg Press

*Prime movers:  Upper and lower legs.*

Starting Position:  Sit in a leg press machine with your back straight. Place your hands on the handlebars and your feet on the support bar.

Lift:

a. With everything remaining still, slowly lower the weight by bending your knees as far as you can.

b.  Explode upward back to the starting position. The entire lift should be in one smooth, fluid motion.

*Tip:  By not lowering the weights down very far, you are able to lift more weights, but will not be training your legs through the entire range of motion.*

## Dead Lift:
### Prime movers: Upper and lower legs.

Starting Position: Stand with your back straight, head tilted back, and leaning slightly forward at the waist. Bend your knees so you can grab a barbell with your arms fully extended.

a. Keeping your arms locked, push with your legs to an upright position. Your lower back will also be used, but try to concentrate on using only your legs to lift the bar off the floor.

b. Slowly lower the bar so that it comes a few inches from the floor, with your arms and back remaining straight and head tilted up.

> *Tip: You may find this exercise easier to perform by gripping the bar with one hand using an overhand grip and the other hand using an underhand grip as shown in the pictures.*

## Leg Extensions
### Prime movers: Upper legs.

Starting Position: Sit with your back straight and hands gripping the handlebars in a leg-extension machine. Place your feet underneath the bar.

Lift:

a. With everything remaining still, raise the bar with your feet by extending your legs as far as you can.

b. Slowly lower your legs back down towards the starting position the same way you brought them up.

> *Tip: If all of the weights on your leg extension/curl machine are still not enough for you, you can perform this exercise one leg at a time.*

## Leg Curls
### Prime movers: Hamstrings

Starting Position: With your back straight and hands gripping the handlebars, lie face down on a leg curl machine and place your feet underneath the bar.

Lift:

a. With everything remaining still, raise the bar with your feet by curling your legs as far as you can.

b. Slowly lower your legs towards the starting position the same way you brought them up.

## Standing Calf Raises
### Prime movers: Calves.

Starting Position: Stand with your shoulders under the supports of a standing calf

raise machine and your toes on the elevated stand provided so that your heels are hanging off the end. Keep your back straight and hands gripping the handlebars.

a. With everything remaining still, stand up on your toes as high as you can Hold the position for a brief moment to maximize the work on your calves.

b. Slowly lower your heels back down towards the starting position the same way you brought them up.

*Tip for all calf raises: To ensure the best workout, raise and lower your heels as high and as low as you can, training your calves through the entire range of motion.*

## Seated Calf Raises
*Prime movers: Calves.*

Starting Position: Sit with your knees under the supports of a standing calf raise machine and your toes on the elevated stand provided so that your heels are hanging off of the stand. Keep your back straight and hands gripping the handlebars.

a. With everything remaining still, rise up on your toes as high as you can. Hold the position for a brief moment to maximize the work on your calves.

b. Slowly lower your heels back down towards the starting position the same way you brought them up.


## Reverse Calf Raises
*Prime movers: Front of lower legs.*

Starting Position: Stand upright with your heels on an elevated stand or block so that your toes are hanging off the stand. This exercise is best performed with no added resistance other than your body weight.

a. With everything remaining still, stand up on your heels as high as you can. Hold the position for a brief moment to maximize the work on the front of your lower legs.

b. Slowly lower your toes back down towards the starting position the same way you brought them up.

## Jump Squats
*Prime movers: Upper and lower legs.*

Starting Position: Stand in a squatting position with your feet shoulder-width apart and your arms crossed over your chest. Keep your back straight and your head tilted up.

Lift:

a. With everything remaining still, explosively jump straight up as high as you can.

b. As you land, return to the starting position in one smooth motion.

## Power Cleans
*Prime movers: Upper and lower legs.*

Starting Position: Stand with your back straight and head titled back. Lean slightly forward at the waist so your shoulders are in front of the bar on the floor. Keep your feet at least shoulder-width apart and your knees bent so you can grab a barbell with your arms fully extended, using an overhand grip.

a. Keeping your arms straight, push with your legs and raise the bar up close to your body to your lower thigh with your knees still slightly bent.

b. From this point, use your lower body for momentum to push yourself straight up while simultaneously using your shoulders to raise the bar to your stomach.

c. In one explosive movement, flip your wrists and elbows underneath the bar while simultaneously jumping into a partial squatting position.

## Box Steps
*Prime movers: Upper and lower legs.*

Starting Position: Stand upright with your feet shoulder-width apart and a barbell resting behind your neck on your traps with your hands slightly wider than shoulder-width apart, using an overhand grip or holding dumbbells at your sides. Keep your back straight and your head tilted up. Stand with a box, bench, or some sort of elevated apparatus in front of you.

a. Step forward up on the box or bench with your right foot. Bring your left knee up so that your left thigh is parallel to the floor.

b. Lower your left leg all the way back down to the floor and bring your right leg back down to meet it. Repeat with other leg.

## Lunges
*Prime movers: Upper and lower legs.*

Starting Position: Stand upright with your feet together and either a barbell resting behind your neck on your traps or holding two dumbbells at your sides as in the picture. Your hands should be slightly wider than shoulder-width apart, using an overhand grip. Keep your back straight and your head tilted up.

Lift:

a. With everything remaining still, slowly take a large step forward with one leg, bending both knees. The weight on your back foot should come up on your toes, and the knee on your back leg should come very close, but not touch the floor.

b. Using your extended leg, thrust yourself back to the starting position the same way you came down. The entire lift should be in one smooth, fluid motion.

> *Tip: The longer your step forward, the more effective this exercise will be.*

# Part IV

# The

# Necessities

# PERFECTING YOUR TECHNIQUE

This section identifies what you need to accomplish before you begin any one of the programs. The information in this section is extremely important for beginners and is also important for experienced weight trainers who have never performed some of the recommended exercises. To follow any type of weight-training routine, you first need to get a feel for the weight room and learn your own strengths.

Now is the time to test out your form, style, and technique. After you have picked the program you would like to follow, be sure to take a day or so to perform warm-up sets with each of the exercises listed in that specific program. The object of these first few sessions is not to train so hard that you are sore the following days, but to practice your form and to gain an understanding for yourself and for the weight room. Simply go to the gym with this book, read the recommended exercises section, and go through a few reps of each exercise using very light weights.

These initial days of practice are very important and can be a major help to you as you progress as a weight trainer and athlete by helping you gain an understanding of approximately how much weight you can handle for each exercise.

## TIP

*You can find one-on-one Sport-Specific e-Training at*
**www.SportsWorkout.com**
*Where you will be matched up with your very own personal trainer who will create customized workouts specifically for you.*

# ESTIMATING YOUR ONE REP MAX

| Tip |
| --- |
| **Your one rep max** *is the greatest amount of weight you can lift at one time or for one repetition for a particular exercise.* |

Knowing your one rep max is an essential part of measuring your strength, your progress, and is very helpful in determining the weight load you should be lifting for every set, regardless of your purpose. This section is called *Estimating* Your One Rep Max because this book never recommends that you *max out*. As discussed in earlier sections, *maxing out* can cause injuries, which, besides being painful and dangerous, can prevent future weight training. *Auxiliary exercises,* or exercises training smaller muscle groups such as biceps and forearms, can be particularly dangerous when trying to max out. With the estimated one rep max chart provided for you, you can estimate your one rep max without having to attempt to lift your max weight. Instead, you can lift a lighter weight several times to safely and accurately estimate what your max is.

Your estimated one rep max for each exercise in an underlying foundation for this book. You will see once you've read through the rest of the text that all of the sets and reps you are required to perform are based on percentages of your estimated one rep max. Depending on your goals, you will be required to lift different percentages of your estimated one rep max.

# Understanding the Chart

## Steps to finding your estimated one rep max:

**1.** Choose an exercise that you want to try to find your estimated one rep max.

**2.**. Choose a test weight that is light enough for you to lift several, but not more than, eight times.

**3.** Lift that weight until failure. If you lift more than eight reps, choose a higher weight and start over.

**4.** Find your test weight on the far left column of the Estimated One-Rep Max Chart.

**5.** Find the number of reps you successfully completed on the top row.

**6.** Scroll right from your test weight and down from your successfully completed reps until you find the number that shares both the same row and column.

### The number you arrive at is your estimated one rep max.

# REPS

| WEIGHT | 1 | 2 | 3 | 4 | 5 | 6 | 7 | 8 |
|---|---|---|---|---|---|---|---|---|
| 5 | 5 | 5 | 5 | 6 | 6 | 6 | 6 | 6 |
| 10 | 10 | 10 | 11 | 11 | 11 | 12 | 12 | 12 |
| 15 | 15 | 15 | 16 | 16 | 17 | 17 | 18 | 19 |
| 20 | 20 | 21 | 21 | 22 | 23 | 23 | 24 | 25 |
| 25 | 25 | 26 | 27 | 27 | 28 | 29 | 30 | 31 |
| 30 | 30 | 31 | 32 | 33 | 34 | 35 | 36 | 37 |
| 35 | 35 | 36 | 37 | 38 | 39 | 41 | 42 | 44 |
| 40 | 40 | 41 | 42 | 44 | 45 | 47 | 48 | 50 |
| 45 | 45 | 46 | 48 | 49 | 51 | 52 | 54 | 56 |
| 50 | 50 | 51 | 53 | 55 | 56 | 58 | 60 | 62 |
| 55 | 55 | 57 | 58 | 60 | 62 | 64 | 66 | 68 |
| 60 | 60 | 62 | 64 | 66 | 68 | 70 | 72 | 75 |
| 65 | 65 | 67 | 69 | 71 | 73 | 76 | 78 | 81 |
| 70 | 70 | 72 | 74 | 76 | 79 | 81 | 84 | 87 |
| 75 | 75 | 77 | 79 | 82 | 84 | 87 | 90 | 93 |
| 80 | 80 | 82 | 85 | 87 | 90 | 93 | 96 | 99 |
| 85 | 85 | 87 | 90 | 93 | 96 | 99 | 102 | 106 |
| 90 | 90 | 93 | 95 | 98 | 101 | 105 | 108 | 112 |
| 95 | 95 | 98 | 101 | 104 | 107 | 110 | 114 | 118 |
| 100 | 100 | 103 | 106 | 109 | 113 | 116 | 120 | 124 |
| 105 | 105 | 108 | 111 | 115 | 118 | 122 | 126 | 130 |
| 110 | 110 | 113 | 117 | 120 | 124 | 128 | 132 | 137 |
| 115 | 115 | 118 | 122 | 126 | 129 | 134 | 138 | 143 |
| 120 | 120 | 123 | 127 | 131 | 135 | 139 | 144 | 149 |

## REPS

| WEIGHT | 1 | 2 | 3 | 4 | 5 | 6 | 7 | 8 |
|---|---|---|---|---|---|---|---|---|
| 125 | 125 | 129 | 132 | 136 | 141 | 145 | 150 | 155 |
| 130 | 130 | 134 | 138 | 142 | 146 | 151 | 156 | 161 |
| 135 | 135 | 139 | 143 | 147 | 152 | 157 | 162 | 168 |
| 140 | 140 | 144 | 148 | 153 | 158 | 163 | 168 | 174 |
| 145 | 145 | 149 | 154 | 158 | 163 | 168 | 174 | 180 |
| 150 | 150 | 154 | 159 | 164 | 169 | 174 | 180 | 186 |
| 155 | 155 | 159 | 164 | 169 | 174 | 180 | 186 | 193 |
| 160 | 160 | 165 | 169 | 175 | 180 | 186 | 192 | 199 |
| 165 | 165 | 170 | 175 | 180 | 186 | 192 | 198 | 205 |
| 170 | 170 | 175 | 180 | 186 | 191 | 197 | 204 | 211 |
| 175 | 175 | 180 | 185 | 191 | 197 | 203 | 210 | 217 |
| 180 | 180 | 185 | 191 | 196 | 203 | 209 | 216 | 224 |
| 185 | 185 | 190 | 196 | 202 | 208 | 215 | 222 | 230 |
| 190 | 190 | 195 | 201 | 207 | 214 | 221 | 228 | 236 |
| 195 | 195 | 201 | 207 | 213 | 219 | 227 | 234 | 242 |
| 200 | 200 | 206 | 212 | 218 | 225 | 232 | 240 | 248 |
| 205 | 205 | 211 | 217 | 224 | 231 | 238 | 246 | 255 |
| 210 | 210 | 216 | 222 | 229 | 236 | 244 | 252 | 261 |
| 215 | 215 | 221 | 228 | 235 | 242 | 250 | 258 | 267 |
| 220 | 220 | 226 | 233 | 240 | 248 | 256 | 264 | 273 |
| 225 | 225 | 231 | 238 | 246 | 253 | 261 | 270 | 279 |
| 230 | 230 | 237 | 244 | 251 | 259 | 267 | 276 | 286 |
| 235 | 235 | 242 | 249 | 256 | 264 | 273 | 282 | 292 |
| 240 | 240 | 247 | 254 | 262 | 270 | 279 | 288 | 298 |

# REPS

| WEIGHT | 1 | 2 | 3 | 4 | 5 | 6 | 7 | 8 |
|---|---|---|---|---|---|---|---|---|
| 245 | 245 | 252 | 259 | 267 | 276 | 285 | 294 | 304 |
| 250 | 250 | 257 | 265 | 273 | 281 | 290 | 300 | 310 |
| 255 | 255 | 262 | 270 | 278 | 287 | 296 | 306 | 317 |
| 260 | 260 | 267 | 275 | 284 | 293 | 302 | 312 | 323 |
| 265 | 265 | 273 | 281 | 289 | 298 | 308 | 318 | 329 |
| 270 | 270 | 278 | 286 | 295 | 304 | 314 | 324 | 335 |
| 275 | 275 | 283 | 291 | 300 | 309 | 319 | 330 | 341 |
| 280 | 280 | 288 | 297 | 306 | 315 | 325 | 336 | 348 |
| 285 | 285 | 293 | 302 | 311 | 321 | 331 | 342 | 354 |
| 290 | 290 | 298 | 307 | 316 | 326 | 337 | 348 | 360 |
| 295 | 295 | 303 | 312 | 322 | 332 | 343 | 354 | 366 |
| 300 | 300 | 309 | 318 | 327 | 338 | 348 | 360 | 373 |
| 305 | 305 | 314 | 323 | 333 | 343 | 354 | 366 | 379 |
| 310 | 310 | 319 | 328 | 338 | 349 | 360 | 372 | 385 |
| 315 | 315 | 324 | 334 | 344 | 354 | 366 | 378 | 391 |
| 320 | 320 | 329 | 339 | 349 | 360 | 372 | 384 | 397 |
| 325 | 325 | 334 | 344 | 355 | 366 | 378 | 390 | 404 |
| 330 | 330 | 339 | 349 | 360 | 371 | 383 | 396 | 410 |
| 335 | 335 | 345 | 355 | 366 | 377 | 389 | 402 | 416 |
| 340 | 340 | 350 | 360 | 371 | 383 | 395 | 408 | 422 |
| 345 | 345 | 355 | 365 | 376 | 388 | 401 | 414 | 428 |
| 350 | 350 | 360 | 371 | 382 | 394 | 407 | 420 | 435 |
| 355 | 355 | 365 | 376 | 387 | 399 | 412 | 426 | 441 |
| 360 | 360 | 370 | 381 | 393 | 405 | 418 | 432 | 447 |

# REPS

| WEIGHT | 1 | 2 | 3 | 4 | 5 | 6 | 7 | 8 |
|---|---|---|---|---|---|---|---|---|
| 365 | 365 | 375 | 387 | 398 | 411 | 424 | 438 | 453 |
| 370 | 370 | 381 | 392 | 404 | 416 | 430 | 444 | 459 |
| 375 | 375 | 386 | 397 | 409 | 422 | 436 | 450 | 466 |
| 380 | 380 | 391 | 402 | 415 | 428 | 441 | 456 | 472 |
| 385 | 385 | 396 | 408 | 420 | 433 | 447 | 462 | 478 |
| 390 | 390 | 401 | 413 | 426 | 439 | 453 | 468 | 484 |
| 395 | 395 | 406 | 418 | 431 | 444 | 459 | 474 | 490 |
| 400 | 400 | 411 | 424 | 436 | 450 | 465 | 480 | 497 |
| 405 | 405 | 417 | 429 | 442 | 456 | 470 | 486 | 503 |
| 410 | 410 | 422 | 434 | 447 | 461 | 476 | 492 | 509 |
| 415 | 415 | 427 | 439 | 453 | 467 | 482 | 498 | 515 |
| 420 | 420 | 432 | 445 | 458 | 473 | 488 | 504 | 522 |
| 425 | 425 | 437 | 450 | 464 | 478 | 494 | 510 | 528 |
| 430 | 430 | 442 | 455 | 469 | 484 | 499 | 516 | 534 |
| 435 | 435 | 447 | 461 | 475 | 489 | 505 | 522 | 540 |
| 440 | 440 | 453 | 466 | 480 | 495 | 511 | 528 | 546 |
| 445 | 445 | 458 | 471 | 486 | 501 | 517 | 534 | 553 |
| 450 | 450 | 463 | 477 | 491 | 506 | 523 | 540 | 559 |
| 455 | 455 | 468 | 482 | 496 | 512 | 529 | 546 | 565 |
| 460 | 460 | 473 | 487 | 502 | 518 | 534 | 552 | 571 |
| 465 | 465 | 478 | 492 | 507 | 523 | 540 | 558 | 577 |
| 470 | 470 | 483 | 498 | 513 | 529 | 546 | 564 | 584 |
| 475 | 475 | 489 | 503 | 518 | 534 | 552 | 570 | 590 |
| 480 | 480 | 494 | 508 | 524 | 540 | 558 | 576 | 596 |

## REPS

| WEIGHT | 1 | 2 | 3 | 4 | 5 | 6 | 7 | 8 |
|---|---|---|---|---|---|---|---|---|
| 485 | 485 | 499 | 514 | 529 | 546 | 563 | 582 | 602 |
| 490 | 490 | 504 | 519 | 535 | 551 | 569 | 588 | 608 |
| 495 | 495 | 509 | 524 | 540 | 557 | 575 | 594 | 615 |
| 500 | 500 | 514 | 529 | 546 | 563 | 581 | 600 | 621 |
| 505 | 505 | 519 | 535 | 551 | 568 | 587 | 606 | 627 |
| 510 | 510 | 525 | 540 | 556 | 574 | 592 | 612 | 633 |
| 515 | 515 | 530 | 545 | 562 | 579 | 598 | 618 | 639 |
| 520 | 520 | 535 | 551 | 567 | 585 | 604 | 624 | 646 |
| 525 | 525 | 540 | 556 | 573 | 591 | 610 | 630 | 652 |
| 530 | 530 | 545 | 561 | 578 | 596 | 616 | 636 | 658 |
| 535 | 535 | 550 | 567 | 584 | 602 | 621 | 642 | 664 |
| 540 | 540 | 555 | 572 | 589 | 608 | 627 | 648 | 671 |
| 545 | 545 | 561 | 577 | 595 | 613 | 633 | 654 | 677 |
| 550 | 550 | 566 | 582 | 600 | 619 | 639 | 660 | 683 |
| 555 | 555 | 571 | 588 | 606 | 624 | 645 | 666 | 689 |
| 560 | 560 | 576 | 593 | 611 | 630 | 650 | 672 | 695 |
| 565 | 565 | 581 | 598 | 616 | 636 | 656 | 678 | 702 |
| 570 | 570 | 586 | 604 | 622 | 641 | 662 | 684 | 708 |
| 575 | 575 | 591 | 609 | 627 | 647 | 668 | 690 | 714 |
| 580 | 580 | 597 | 614 | 633 | 653 | 674 | 696 | 720 |
| 585 | 585 | 602 | 619 | 638 | 658 | 679 | 702 | 726 |
| 590 | 590 | 607 | 625 | 644 | 664 | 685 | 708 | 733 |
| 595 | 595 | 612 | 630 | 649 | 669 | 691 | 714 | 739 |
| 600 | 600 | 617 | 635 | 655 | 675 | 697 | 720 | 745 |

# THE DIFFERENT FOLKS, DIFFERENT STROKES PRINCIPLE

As the title of this section indicates, not everyone is the same. In weight training, differences can occur both physically and psychologically. Some people are born with greater muscle-building capabilities than others. A major reason for these genetic differences is the amount of fast-twitch muscle fibers one has. Fast-twitch fibers are able to grow bigger and stronger than the other muscle fibers. Do not feel frustrated if you see others making faster initial gains than you are, because you can and will make enormous gains by following any one of the provided programs. By sticking with your routine and working hard, you can catch and surpass almost everyone. Fast-twitch, as well as slow-twitch fibers, are explained in further detail in the section *Muscle Fibers*.

Weight trainers also differ mentally and psychologically. Different people have different preferences in terms of how they like to work out, what exercises they like to do, as well as how often they like to train. Many of the various programs in this book are based on contrasting styles of equally legitimate training principles. Some programs are for strength and bulk building, others for power enhancement, and still others for increasing endurance, stamina, and burning fat.

**Overtraining** *is when you work out so hard that your training negatively affects your goals.*

# OVERTRAINING AND STALENESS

*Your muscles need at least forty-eight hours to fully recover from weight training, which is why you should never train the same muscle groups on consecutive days.*

Everyone, at one point or another, reaches a plateau in his or her training. When this happens, gains are very hard to come by. Many times plateaus occur because of overtraining. Overtraining can occur during one workout, or it can gradually creep up on you over time. It is important to push yourself as hard as you can in the gym and make the most of your time, but there can be a time when you are doing too much. Training seven days a week is an example of overtraining. We all need rest days so our muscles can recoup, regroup, and rebuild. It is during these days off that your body is able to grow bigger and stronger. None of our programs requires you to lift all seven days of the week because it would not allow enough time for your muscles to fully recover. Even the biggest and strongest athletes, body builders, and weight lifters take at least one day of rest per week.

During one session, some people are able to work out for hours without overtraining, while others simply can't handle that much physical stress. Most beginners will not be able to work out for as long or as often as more experienced weight trainers because their bodies are not yet prepared for that type of strenuous work.

Staleness, on the other hand, is thought by many experts to be a response to overtraining. It is a syndrome that negatively affects your athletic performance and your personality. Rest is the only method of prevention and the only cure for staleness. The programs provided for you all have been designed so that there is a minimal chance of overtraining and staleness occurring; however, if you do begin to notice symptoms, take at least one week off from weight training and see your physician.

## Symptoms of staleness include:

**1.**    Reaching a plateau in training gains

**2.**    Having unusual sleeping patterns

**3.**    Performing tasks seems more difficult

**4.**    Having a decreased appetite leading to unhealthy lean body weight loss

**5.**    Having increased irritability and anxiety

**6.**    Experiencing depression

**7.**    Having a decreased sex drive

Endurance athletes are at the greatest risk of staleness; however, all athletes should be aware of this syndrome regardless of the sport. The different folks, different strokes principle applies to staleness. Many athletes may never experience staleness, but everyone needs to be aware that it can happen.

# THE DECLARATION OF VARIATION

Variation is introducing some sort of change in your workout routine. It can be the constant changing of exercises within a program or the compete changing of your program every few weeks. Variation is very important in weight training for several physiological and psychological reasons. Some of the most important benefits of variation in a weight-training program include:

**1.     Not allowing your body to adapt to any one routine:** Perhaps the most important reason to vary your routines is so you can keep making progress and gains. Variation is the key to continued progress. Your body is a machine designed to adapt to any stress placed on it, whether it be heat, pressure, or tension. Similarly, your body adapts to the workload you are putting on it in the gym. After following the same routine for long enough, you will plateau because your body has become used to and has adapted to doing the same thing over and over again. When a plateau occurs, you need to shock your body with different types of stimuli to continue making gains. By occasionally switching the type of training you do (how many reps, sets, exercises, and their order), you shock your body so that it has to readapt to the new workload you are putting on it, which enables you to continue to progress.

**2.     Keeping you from getting bored:** Following the same routine day after day can become very boring and tiresome. Fitness experts and coaches alike know that boredom in the gym can be a major problem for athletes and other weight trainers. In order to make big gains, you need to train hard and with intensity. Once that intensity is lost, so are the benefits from training hard. When people are bored with their routine, they lose motivation and train with less passion. It is human nature. Unfortunately, this lack of motivation spawns a negative cycle. By not training as hard, gains become more difficult, thus leading to an even greater decrease in motivation, which leads again to not training hard. And so the cycle continues. Varying exercises and styles every so often keeps things fresh and keeps people motivated, especially athletes in the midst of a long off-season. For these reasons, each of the programs in the back of the book last for only four weeks with slight changes occurring after two weeks.

**3.      Targeting, strengthening, and toning every part of every muscle:** As you've noticed, this book provides you with many weight-training exercises. Many of these exercises train the same muscle groups. Like people, no two exercises are exactly alike. Some may be similar, but not identical. Each exercise targets your muscle from a different angle and achieves a different benefit. By using a variety of exercises on the same muscles, you strengthen every part of those muscles. It is the key to really defining your entire body, providing you with more explosive power for athletic events, and creating nice separation between muscle groups.

It is the idea of variation that makes this book what it is. Variation is the reason this book includes 54 different programs each designed for different purposes.

# MUSCLE FIBERS

(How to Train, What and Why)

Our muscles are made up of many bundles of muscle fibers. Each fiber type has its own characteristics and purposes. For simplicity purposes, these muscle fibers can be categorized as:

1.   **Fast-Twitch Fibers**

2.   **Slow-Twitch Fibers**

3.   **Intermediate Fibers (properties of both)**

The muscle-fiber makeup in most people is roughly 25% fast twitch, 25% slow twitch, and 50% intermediate fibers, which contain properties of both fast- and slow-twitch muscle fibers. With proper training some of the intermediate fibers can be converted to fast- or slow–twitch fibers. The more fast-twitch fibers one has, the more powerful and explosive he or she will be. People with more slow-twitch fibers will have greater endurance and stamina. Depending on your purpose, you can weight train in order to build up either muscle fiber.

## Fast-Twitch Fibers

Generally, fast-twitch fibers are used in strength and explosive sports or sports that require bursts of speed and power for relatively short amounts of time. A running back bursting through a hole, a baseball or softball player trying to beat out an infield hit, a basketball player exploding up to the hoop for a slam, a golfer ripping a drive three hundred yards off the tee, a tennis player smashing a backhand across the court, a short distance swimmer torpedoing through the water, and a 110 hurdler flying down the lane are all putting their fast-twitch fibers to the test. Any type of explosive movement is being performed by fast-twitch fibers. People who participate in these or similar types of activities should concentrate primarily on working their fast-twitch fibers

The simple reason more fast-twitch muscle fibers lead to better performance in explosive activities is because they contract faster and with more power than slow-twitch fibers. Fast-twitch fibers lead to *hypertrophy*—an increase in the size of muscle fibers as an outcome of weight training—more easily than slow-twitch fibers. As your muscle fibers increase in size, so do your muscles. The downside to fast-twitch fibers is that they can only work at full capacity for short periods of time before fatiguing because they work primarily without oxygen, or *anaerobically*, and get most of their energy from limited stores of muscle glycogen.

## Slow-Twitch Fibers

Slow-twitch fibers are used in stamina and endurance-based activities. Long distance runners, cyclists, swimmers, and triathletes are examples of people who should concentrate on slow-twitch training. Slow-twitch fibers contract more slowly than fast-twitch fibers, but are able to work for hours longer if trained properly. Slow-twitch fibers get their energy aerobically, from oxygen. Slow-twitch training is great for burning fat because oxygen stimulates the use of fat for energy. There is less hypertrophy in slow-twitch fibers, which is why marathon runners tend to be much smaller than football players.

# TRAINING TECHNIQUES

### Training to Failure:

Training to failure means training in a particular set until you exhaust yourself and cannot complete another repetition on your own. Whether you are training for endurance, power, or strength, it is recommended that you train to failure in most of your sets. By training to failure, you train your body to its maximum capabilities. This type of training is tough, but well worth the results.

### Forced Reps:

Forced reps are performed directly after you have trained to positive failure and cannot complete another repetition. You lower the weight regularly and your partner helps you slowly lift it back up. Your partner should assist you to complete the rep, but not do all of the work for you. Your partner should make sure you spend at least three or four seconds on the positive phase of the lift while assisting you.

### Negatives:

Negatives are also performed directly after you have trained to failure. The opposite of forced reps, the eccentric, or lowering aspect of the lift, is extremely slow, and the concentric part of the lift is fast, with the help of your partner. It should take you approximately six or seven seconds to lower the weights with the help of your partner. At this point, with the help from a spotter, quickly return the weights to their starting position and repeat. Using negatives is the best method for increasing strength and size; however, they should not be used very often because they work your muscles so hard they need over a week in order to fully recover before performing them again.

> *You are able to perform negatives with weights higher than your one rep max because eccentrically you can l ift a great deal more than you can concentrically.*

## Supersets:

This is a training method where you perform one set of two exercises sequentially without rest. For example, if you were to superset preacher curls with triceps curls, you would do one set of preachers and immediately after completion, do one set of triceps curls and then rest before repeating.

## Tri Sets:

Same as Supersets but with three exercises instead of two.

## Pre-exhaust:

This method is one of the most intense methods of weight training. It is a form of supersetting where you perform many reps of a single-joint exercise and immediately follow it up with a compound exercise training the same muscles. For example, if you were to pre-exhaust your shoulders, you would first perform many reps of light lateral raises and immediately follow it up with a military press.

## Burnouts (stripping method):

This method is very popular and very effective. Directly after you complete a set working to failure, immediately lighten the load of the weights so you can continue to train without rest, and perform the next set to failure where you will again lighten the load and work to failure.

## Pyramid Method:

The pyramid method is a great strength-building tactic. It is performed properly by decreasing the reps and increasing the weight with every set. An example would be performing five reps with 100 lbs. followed by three reps with 120 lbs. and one rep with 140 lbs.

## 21 s:

This method is most often performed for biceps exercises, particularly for preacher curls. These exercises are properly executed by performing seven reps going from the bottom of the lift to the halfway point and back for seven reps, then performing seven reps going from the halfway point to the top, followed by seven reps through the complete range of motion.

## Cycling:

Cycling is rotating between two or three different routines. As long as the routines are different, it is considered cycling. A holistic cycle would be following an endurance program, then a power program, and then a strength program. It is best to take one week of active or complete rest after you have completed a full cycle to let your body completely recover before beginning again. Active rest is any sort of low-level, non-structured activity.

## Circuit Training:

Circuit training is the best method of weight training for total fitness and aerobic benefits. It is a great way to get a fast and effective full-body workout. Circuit training is a type of endurance training in which you perform one set of six to ten exercises consecutively without rest. The six to ten exercises should train the major muscle groups of your entire body for a complete workout. After you have completed one circuit through the entire rotation, rest for a short time before repeating.

# WHEN TO INCREASE

(The X + 3 Method)

> **Rule of Thumb:** *Increase the number of reps before increasing the weight,*

The goal of weight training is to gradually increase the resistance over time. Two ways of increasing the resistance are:

## 1. Increasing the weight

## 2. Increasing the number of reps

Increasing the weight you lift can be overwhelming and difficult, so this book recommends that once a weight begins to feel too light for the designated number of repetitions, increase the number of reps before increasing the weight. The X + 3 method states that if you are required to lift X reps in a given set and are able to accomplish it, then the next time you lift, go for X + 1 reps using the same weight. As each exercise begins to feel lighter and lighter, increase your reps up until X + 3. When reps of X + 3 become easily attainable, increase the weight by 5 lbs. and return to reps of X, repeating this entire process. While training smaller, auxiliary-muscle groups like your biceps, triceps and forearms, make increases by 2 pounds at a time. Below is an example of the X + 3 method.

Your routine requires you to bench 100 lbs. 10 times. You complete the 10 reps with ease and the next time you go to the gym you lifts 100 lbs. 11 times. You continue this process until benching 100 lbs. 13 times becomes easy. At this point, you increase your bench to 105 lbs. and start back with 10 reps.

# Choosing the Right Program

Provided for you are 54 programs/routines. Each one is designed for a different purpose. How do you know which one to choose? Below are important factors to consider when selecting your program:

## Purpose:

The most important factor to consider when choosing your program is the purpose for which you are training. Do you want to get bigger, stronger, more toned, more powerful, leaner, or do you want to train for general fitness? If you want to get big and choose an endurance program, you will be working away from your goal. Make sure you choose a program that fits your purpose.

## Weight-Training Experience:

The second factor to consider while choosing your program is your experience in the gym. For each style of training, you are offered different levels of intensity. If you are a beginner, you probably want to start out with a program of less time and frequency than the more advanced programs provided so you do not run the risk of overtraining. Likewise, if you are experienced in weight training and are looking to take the next step, you will most likely follow a program with more exercises and greater frequency to get a better workout.

## Time Availability:

Your time availability is also a major factor in determining your program. You are provided with programs ranging from three to six days per week. For each style, you can choose between six levels of difficulty based on the amount of exercises and the frequency of your training. If you do not have much time to train, then choose a Level I or Level II program. If you have a lot of time to train and have the desire to train hard, then choose a Level IV or Level V program. Level VI programs are recommended only for the very advanced weight trainers. Assuming you train with the same intensity, you will see results faster by training with a more difficult program.

## Personal Preference

This is the final element you should use while determining your program. The next section explains your choices.

# PERSONAL PREFERENCE

Once you have found all of the programs that meet your criteria in terms of purpose, experience, and time availability, you can make your final decision based on your personal preference. Take a look at each of the programs and decide which style of training you like more. You can choose between training *antagonistic* (opposite) muscle groups or *synergistic* (goal-congruent) muscle groups on the same day. These are the two major styles of weight training. Both are excellent ways of working out and are used equally by numerous athletes, body builders, and weight lifters. The styles are:

## Antagonistic (Opposite) Muscle Training

**Pros:** By training antagonistic muscle groups on the same day, you are stretching your muscles and increasing your flexibility and range of motion. For example, while training your triceps, you are extending your arm, which stretches your biceps. You can become very flexible by using this style of training and stretching during your cooling down period.

### Examples of antagonistic-muscle groups include:

Biceps/Triceps

Chest/Lats (Back)

Hamstrings/Quadriceps (thighs)

Abdominals/Lower Back

**Cons:** The major problem that arises from this style of training is fatigue. The larger the muscle group you are training, the more fatigued you will become. When training antagonistic muscle groups, you will train your chest and your lats (back) on the same day. These are both very large muscle groups, and, if you are training hard, you may experience some fatigue.

> *The larger the muscle group you are training,*
> *the more fatigued you will get.*

## Synergistic (Goal-Congruent) Muscle Training: "The Push-Pull Method"

**Pros:** Training synergistically allows you to train your muscles with even greater focus because every exercise you perform will be training at least one common muscle. Examples of synergistic training include training your chest and triceps on the same day because they both work out the triceps. Another example of this is working your lats (back) and your biceps, both training your biceps. This type of training is referred to as the *push-pull method* because you will be performing all of your pushing exercises on one day and all of your pulling exercises on the next.

**Cons:** The only true cost of training this way is that you do not get the stretch in your muscles during your weight-training session as you do in opposite-muscle training. If your sport requires serious flexibility, you may be better off training with the antagonistic muscle approach.

> *It is best if you periodically switch from one style to the*
> *next to shock your body with a different type of training. Try*
> *out both of the major styles of training and determine for*
> *yourself what works best for you.*

# PROGRAM LEVELS

All of the programs are broken down into six levels of difficulty. The least intense programs are Level I for beginners or for people without much time to spend in the gym. The most intense programs are Level VI, which are to be used exclusively by experienced weight trainers looking to take their training to the next stage. The Level I programs have been created to be easier on your body while still allowing you to make progress, and the Level VI programs have been created to train you as hard as possible without overtraining. The more intense the program, the faster you will see results.

**Level I:** Beginners

**Level II:** Somewhat intense

**Level III:** Moderate intensity

**Level IV:** Above average intensity

**Level V:** Very intense

**Level VI:** Extremely Intense — Recommended only for experienced weight trainers.

The program levels are not based on how hard you train while in the gym. The levels are based on three other factors:

1. **Frequency**

2. **Time**

3. **Advanced training methods**

**Frequency:** The programs provided for you are either three or four days per week, allowing you to increase them up to six days per week—except strength-training programs, which must not exceed five days per week. Therefore, the more frequent the program has you working out, the greater the total intensity of the program.

*Three-days–a-week programs:* Our least frequent programs require you to train three days per week. Anything less would not be enough training for you to make gains. Training twice a week is considered to be *maintenance training*, allowing you to do nothing more than maintain the gains you have already made.

Each one of the three-days-a-week programs trains your entire body in one session and can be performed by circuit training if you desire. Circuit training is explained in more detail in *Training Techniques*. Because you are training your entire body in one session, you are not able to put much focus on any one muscle group. Training a minimum of three days a week ensures that you are working every muscle in your body the required number of times per week to continue making gains. Also, because you are training your entire body during one session, the following day is always a rest day, providing your muscles with sufficient time to recoup and regroup.

*Four-plus-days-a-week programs:* As the frequency of the program grows, so do the choices. When you train more than three days per week, you cannot train your entire body in one single day because you would not be able to take a day of rest after every training session. With these more frequent programs, you can choose whether you want to follow a two- or three-day split. Training different muscle groups each day gives your muscles time to rest while other muscles are being trained, enabling you to train in consecutive days. Notice that you are never required to train all seven days of the week because your body needs at least one full day of rest to heal and grow stronger.

*If you choose to increase the frequency of your prescribed program, bump up its level of difficulty by one.*

**Time:** Certain programs contain more exercises than others. The number of required exercises relates directly to the time you will be spending in the gym. The more exercises the program has, the higher the intensity level will be.

**Advanced-training methods:** The last factor determining the level of the program is the use of advanced-training methods. These methods include negatives, supersets, forced reps, pre-exhausts, and burnouts, which are explained in further detail in the next section.

## Tip

*These methods are optional throughout each program. The use of advanced training methods moves the difficulty of the program up one level.*

These methods are optional throughout each program. The use of advanced training methods moves the difficulty of the program up one level.

Each of the programs is designed for you to make serious gains and positive changes to your body, mind, health, and athletic ability. The more intense the program, the quicker you will be able to achieve and surpass your goals. The harder you train, the faster your muscles will respond. These programs have been carefully created so that you do not over- or undertrain yourself based on principles regarding sufficient time to rest and train your muscles.

# SAFETY REMINDERS

When done properly, weight training can be a very effective way to sculpt your body and achieve your athletic potential. On top of all of the performance-enhancing benefits to weight training, it also plays a major role in injury reduction, injury prevention, and injury rehabilitation. With stronger muscles supporting your bones, tendons, and ligaments, you will be much less injury prone and will able to perform most activities hard and strong all the time. However, if necessary safety precautions are not followed, injuries can result.

## Listed below are a few safety reminders to help keep you injury free in the gym.

**Always use a spotter:** It does not matter how experienced you are or how light you think the weight is, you always need someone to spot you.

**Use safety collars:** Collars will prevent weights from tipping over during a lift, which can result in an injury to you or others.

**Pick up weights properly:** Most injuries in the weight room come from picking up and putting weights down improperly. To avoid chronic lower-back problems, be sure to bend at the knees and to keep your back straight every time you pick up or put down weights.

**Drink enough water:** Even if you are not thirsty, be sure to drink lots of water before and during your workout, especially if you anticipate a lot of perspiration. As you become dehydrated, your ability to perform work drops way off, which will limit your intensity and slow your progress.

**Use proper form:** Proper form will provide you with the best results and help keep you injury free.

**Breathe correctly:** It is very important to simply breathe while performing any exercise, inhaling on the negative part of the lift and exhaling on the positive part. Do not hold your breath!

**Do not drop weights:** Not only can this break the weights, but it can also be very dangerous for everyone in the gym. Always put the weights back in a controlled manner.

**Dress properly:** Gym shoes are a must; wearing inappropriate gym attire like sandals can results in injuries such as broken toes.

**Use your head:** If you begin to feel sick, queasy, light-headed, or if you experience joint or chest pains, stop your session and get yourself checked out immediately.

**Consult your physician:** It is required for everyone to check with his or her physician before beginning any one of the prescribed programs or before increasing the intensity to any of the programs.

# RECORD KEEPING

When following any type of program, it is vital that you keep daily records for many reasons. Five of the most important are:

1. **Knowing when to increase the weight or reps**

2. **Knowing where to start after taking time away from the gym**

3. **Observing your gains over time**

4. **Motivation**

5. **Detect overtraining**

You can keep records on any or all of a vast number of factors that may be important to your training or progress. You have been provided with an example of a record-keeping chart to help you monitor your progress. You can print an unlimited amount of these charts from www.sportsworkout.com/chart.htm. They have been made accessible so you can keep records in the very best and easiest way possible. To complement the record-keeping chart, there is a testing sheet, which can also be printed from the Web site at www.sportsworkout.com/test.htm. With the testing sheets, you will be able to use formulas to literally put your strength, power, endurance, and athletic ability to the test.

> *You can find well-designed printable record-keeping charts at* **www.sportsworkout.com/chart.htm** *that are designed to work with any one of the provided routines, and testing sheets at* **www.sportsworkout.com/test.htm** *where you can test your progress in many fashions.*

**When to increase:** Keeping records of your daily activity in the gym will allow you to determine when you are ready to increase the workload and by how much. Without well-kept records, your attempts to intensify your weight-training regimen will be made with hit or miss tactics. These tactics are not efficient ways to make gains because you will waste time by approximating your weight-loads and you may not be pushing yourself hard enough with the proper resistance. With well-kept records, you will know exactly when you need to increase the load and by how much.

**Where to start:** At one point or another, there will be instances when you will be unable to make it to the gym for extended periods of time. It may be because you become ill, experience a death in the family, or go on a vacation. The bottom line is there may be a time when you will stop your program and need to re-enter it. By keeping records, you will know exactly where you left off. Because you have taken time away from lifting, however, you will need to slightly decrease the load from where you left off, but you will have your records as a measuring stick. This is a very important aspect to training. If you take an extended period of time away from lifting without maintaining records, you will have to go by memory, which will result in trial and error once again.

**Observe your gains:** It is very important to be able to observe your gains for several reasons. The most important is that with well-kept records, you will be able to see which parts of the body you have made improvements in and which parts still need work. The records give you a sense of what changes need to be made for your next program to make up for these differences. You will want to saturate your next program with more exercises that train the weaker areas of your body, and this information can only be known with well-kept records.

**Motivation:** On top of monitoring your progress in the gym, record keeping provides you with the motivation to continue working harder and making bigger gains. You will literally be able to see on paper how you have progressed over time, which will inspire you to want to train harder. When people have hard evidence that they are actually making gains in the gym, it motivates them to continue making those gains.

**Overtraining:** How are record keeping and overtraining related? Even if you do not feel overtrained, you will be able to clearly see if you are overtrained by looking at your records. If, over time, you notice decreases from one day to the next in your records, the culprit may be overtraining. Overtraining may not always be the reason, but it very well could be. Other reasons could be changes in your eating or sleeping pattern or illness. In any case, record keeping will help you determine what the problem may be and how you can fix it.

Larger printable record keeping charts can be found at
**www.SportsWorkout.com/chart.htm**

**Top Left Chart**

| DATE: | | BODY WT: | Hours of Sleep: | | | | |
|---|---|---|---|---|---|---|---|
| Time IN: | Time OUT: | Other: | | | | | |
| | | Set 1 | Set 2 | Set 3 | Set 4 | Set 5 | |
| EXERCISE: | WEIGHT | | | | | | |
| | DESIRED REPS | | | | | | |
| | COMPLETED REPS | | | | | | |
| EXERCISE: | WEIGHT | | | | | | |
| | DESIRED REPS | | | | | | |
| | COMPLETED REPS | | | | | | |
| EXERCISE: | WEIGHT | | | | | | |
| | DESIRED REPS | | | | | | |
| | COMPLETED REPS | | | | | | |
| EXERCISE: | WEIGHT | | | | | | |
| | DESIRED REPS | | | | | | |
| | COMPLETED REPS | | | | | | |
| EXERCISE: | WEIGHT | | | | | | |
| | DESIRED REPS | | | | | | |
| | COMPLETED REPS | | | | | | |
| EXERCISE: | WEIGHT | | | | | | |
| | DESIRED REPS | | | | | | |
| | COMPLETED REPS | | | | | | |
| EXERCISE: | WEIGHT | | | | | | |
| | DESIRED REPS | | | | | | |
| | COMPLETED REPS | | | | | | |

**Top Right Chart**

| DATE: | | BODY WT: | Hours of Sleep: | | | | |
|---|---|---|---|---|---|---|---|
| Time IN: | Time OUT: | Other: | | | | | |
| | | Set 1 | Set 2 | Set 3 | Set 4 | Set 5 | |
| EXERCISE: | WEIGHT | | | | | | |
| | DESIRED REPS | | | | | | |
| | COMPLETED REPS | | | | | | |
| EXERCISE: | WEIGHT | | | | | | |
| | DESIRED REPS | | | | | | |
| | COMPLETED REPS | | | | | | |
| EXERCISE: | WEIGHT | | | | | | |
| | DESIRED REPS | | | | | | |
| | COMPLETED REPS | | | | | | |
| EXERCISE: | WEIGHT | | | | | | |
| | DESIRED REPS | | | | | | |
| | COMPLETED REPS | | | | | | |
| EXERCISE: | WEIGHT | | | | | | |
| | DESIRED REPS | | | | | | |
| | COMPLETED REPS | | | | | | |
| EXERCISE: | WEIGHT | | | | | | |
| | DESIRED REPS | | | | | | |
| | COMPLETED REPS | | | | | | |
| EXERCISE: | WEIGHT | | | | | | |
| | DESIRED REPS | | | | | | |
| | COMPLETED REPS | | | | | | |

**Bottom Left Chart**

| DATE: | | BODY WT: | Hours of Sleep: | | | | |
|---|---|---|---|---|---|---|---|
| Time IN: | Time OUT: | Other: | | | | | |
| | | Set 1 | Set 2 | Set 3 | Set 4 | Set 5 | |
| EXERCISE: | WEIGHT | | | | | | |
| | DESIRED REPS | | | | | | |
| | COMPLETED REPS | | | | | | |
| EXERCISE: | WEIGHT | | | | | | |
| | DESIRED REPS | | | | | | |
| | COMPLETED REPS | | | | | | |
| EXERCISE: | WEIGHT | | | | | | |
| | DESIRED REPS | | | | | | |
| | COMPLETED REPS | | | | | | |
| EXERCISE: | WEIGHT | | | | | | |
| | DESIRED REPS | | | | | | |
| | COMPLETED REPS | | | | | | |
| EXERCISE: | WEIGHT | | | | | | |
| | DESIRED REPS | | | | | | |
| | COMPLETED REPS | | | | | | |
| EXERCISE: | WEIGHT | | | | | | |
| | DESIRED REPS | | | | | | |
| | COMPLETED REPS | | | | | | |
| EXERCISE: | WEIGHT | | | | | | |
| | DESIRED REPS | | | | | | |
| | COMPLETED REPS | | | | | | |

**Bottom Right Chart**

| DATE: | | BODY WT: | Hours of Sleep: | | | | |
|---|---|---|---|---|---|---|---|
| Time IN: | Time OUT: | Other: | | | | | |
| | | Set 1 | Set 2 | Set 3 | Set 4 | Set 5 | |
| EXERCISE: | WEIGHT | | | | | | |
| | DESIRED REPS | | | | | | |
| | COMPLETED REPS | | | | | | |
| EXERCISE: | WEIGHT | | | | | | |
| | DESIRED REPS | | | | | | |
| | COMPLETED REPS | | | | | | |
| EXERCISE: | WEIGHT | | | | | | |
| | DESIRED REPS | | | | | | |
| | COMPLETED REPS | | | | | | |
| EXERCISE: | WEIGHT | | | | | | |
| | DESIRED REPS | | | | | | |
| | COMPLETED REPS | | | | | | |
| EXERCISE: | WEIGHT | | | | | | |
| | DESIRED REPS | | | | | | |
| | COMPLETED REPS | | | | | | |
| EXERCISE: | WEIGHT | | | | | | |
| | DESIRED REPS | | | | | | |
| | COMPLETED REPS | | | | | | |
| EXERCISE: | WEIGHT | | | | | | |
| | DESIRED REPS | | | | | | |
| | COMPLETED REPS | | | | | | |

# TEST YOURSELF!

By testing yourself, you can visually see the gains you have made, and how extensive they have been. Provided for you at www.sportsworkout.com/test.htm are strength, power, endurance, and sport-specific tests so you can measure your progress in every fashion. You can also keep track of other important variables such as body weight, as well as muscle and waistline measurements.

> ▶ *Retest yourself every six weeks to monitor your gains.*

You can apply the strength, power, or endurance tests to any and all of the recommended exercises. However, it is suggested that you only test yourself in the bench press, leg press, military press, and lat pull because it would take days for you to test yourself in each of the recommended exercises. These four exercises are good indications of your overall fitness because they cover all of your major muscle groups. The bench press works your chest and triceps. The leg press covers your entire lower body. The lat pull has you working your lats and biceps. And military press trains your shoulders and traps.

The website provides you with several ways of testing yourself so that you will know exactly what you have improved in and what you may still need work on. For every non-weight-training related test, take the best of three tests to ensure the most accurate results.

# CONCLUSION

You are now ready to begin weight training. You have all of the information in front of you and expert-designed programs for your use, equipping you with the best methods available to improve your athletic potential. You also know how to apply the exercises properly. With hard work and determination, you will achieve any goals you set for yourself. Best of luck training.

To further maximize your training, be sure to sign up for our Sport-Specific e-Training Program by going to www. SportsWorkout.com for one-on-one online training and customized workouts from personal trainers.

# Part V

# Supplemental

# 4-Week

# Programs

# Endurance/
# Fat Burning
# Training

# Endurance/Fat Burning Training
Entire body every training day
Rest every other day

## Weeks 1 and 2

| Day 1 | | | Day 2 | | | Day 3 | | |
|---|---|---|---|---|---|---|---|---|

**Day 1**

| exercise | sets | reps |
|---|---|---|
| barbell bench press | 3 | 20 |
| seated cable rows | 3 | 20 |
| squats | 3 | 20 |
| dumbbell military press | 3 | 20 |

**Day 2**

| exercise | sets | reps |
|---|---|---|
| incline barbell bench press | 3 | 20 |
| one arm dumbbell rows | 3 | 20 |
| leg press | 3 | 20 |
| barbell military press | 3 | 20 |

**Day 3**

| exercise | sets | reps |
|---|---|---|
| barbell bench press | 3 | 20 |
| seated cable rows | 3 | 20 |
| squats | 3 | 20 |
| dumbbell military press | 3 | 20 |

## Weeks 3 and 4

**Day 1**

| exercise | sets | reps |
|---|---|---|
| barbell bench press | 3 | 25 |
| seated cable rows | 3 | 25 |
| squats | 3 | 25 |
| dumbbell military press | 3 | 25 |

**Day 2**

| exercise | sets | reps |
|---|---|---|
| incline barbell bench press | 3 | 25 |
| one arm dumbbell rows | 3 | 25 |
| leg press | 3 | 25 |
| barbell military press | 3 | 25 |

**Day 3**

| exercise | sets | reps |
|---|---|---|
| barbell bench press | 3 | 25 |
| seated cable rows | 3 | 25 |
| squats | 3 | 25 |
| dumbbell military press | 3 | 25 |

Program Level II
# Endurance/Fat Burning Training
Entire body every training day
Rest every other day

## Weeks 1 and 2

**Day 1**

| exercise | sets | reps |
|---|---|---|
| barbell bench press | 3 | 20 |
| seated cable rows | 3 | 20 |
| squats | 3 | 20 |
| dumbbell military press | 3 | 20 |
| lunges | 3 | 20 |
| front raises | 2 | 20 |

**Day 2**

| exercise | sets | reps |
|---|---|---|
| dumbbell bench press | 3 | 20 |
| standing flyes | 3 | 20 |
| bent-over barbell rows | 3 | 20 |
| leg curls | 3 | 20 |
| standing calf raises | 3 | 20 |
| cable crossovers | 2 | 20 |

**Day 3**

| exercise | sets | reps |
|---|---|---|
| barbell bench press | 3 | 20 |
| seated cable rows | 3 | 20 |
| squats | 3 | 20 |
| dumbbell military press | 3 | 20 |
| lunges | 3 | 20 |
| front raises | 2 | 20 |

## Weeks 3 and 4

**Day 1**

| exercise | sets | reps |
|---|---|---|
| barbell bench press | 3 | 25 |
| seated cable rows | 3 | 25 |
| squats | 3 | 25 |
| dumbbell military press | 3 | 25 |
| lunges | 3 | 25 |
| front raises | 2 | 25 |

**Day 2**

| exercise | sets | reps |
|---|---|---|
| dumbbell bench press | 3 | 25 |
| standing flyes | 3 | 25 |
| bent-over barbell rows | 3 | 25 |
| leg curls | 3 | 25 |
| standing calf raises | 3 | 25 |
| cable crossovers | 2 | 25 |

**Day 3**

| exercise | sets | reps |
|---|---|---|
| barbell bench press | 3 | 25 |
| seated cable rows | 3 | 25 |
| squats | 3 | 25 |
| dumbbell military press | 3 | 25 |
| lunges | 3 | 25 |
| front raises | 2 | 25 |

## Program Level II
# Endurance/Fat Burning Training
Three-Day Split four days a week
Antagonistic Training

## Weeks 1 and 2

**Day 1**

| exercise | sets | reps |
| --- | --- | --- |
| barbell bench press | 3 | 20 |
| dumbbell incline bench press | 2 | 20 |
| seated cable rows | 3 | 20 |
| bent-over barbell rows | 2 | 20 |

**Day 2**

| exercise | sets | reps |
| --- | --- | --- |
| triceps kickbacks | 2 | 20 |
| bench dips | 2 | 20 |
| dumbbell curls | 2 | 20 |
| incline curls | 2 | 20 |

**Day 3**

| exercise | sets | reps |
| --- | --- | --- |
| squats | 3 | 20 |
| leg curls | 2 | 20 |
| dumbbell military press | 3 | 20 |
| upright rows | 3 | 20 |

## Weeks 3 and 4

**Day 1**

| exercise | sets | reps |
| --- | --- | --- |
| dumbbell bench press | 3 | 25 |
| incline barbell bench press | 2 | 25 |
| one-arm dumbbell rows | 3 | 25 |
| T-bar rows | 2 | 25 |

**Day 2**

| exercise | sets | reps |
| --- | --- | --- |
| preacher curls | 2 | 25 |
| reverse curls | 2 | 25 |
| barbell triceps curls | 2 | 25 |
| bench dips | 2 | 25 |

**Day 3**

| exercise | sets | reps |
| --- | --- | --- |
| leg press | 3 | 25 |
| lunges | 3 | 25 |
| barbell military press | 3 | 25 |
| front raises | 2 | 25 |

## Program Level II
# Endurance/Fat Burning Training
Three-Day Split four days a week
Synergistic Training

## Weeks 1 and 2

**Day 1**

| exercise | sets | reps |
| --- | --- | --- |
| dumbbell bench press | 3 | 20 |
| incline barbell bench press | 3 | 20 |
| triceps kickbacks | 2 | 20 |
| bench dips | 2 | failure |

**Day 2**

| exercise | sets | reps |
| --- | --- | --- |
| seated cable rows | 3 | 20 |
| bent-over barbell rows | 3 | 20 |
| dumbbell curls | 2 | 20 |
| incline curls | 2 | 20 |

**Day 3**

| exercise | sets | reps |
| --- | --- | --- |
| squats | 3 | 20 |
| leg extensions | 2 | 20 |
| dumbbell military press | 3 | 20 |
| upright rows | 3 | 20 |

## Weeks 3 and 4

**Day 1**

| exercise | sets | reps |
| --- | --- | --- |
| barbell bench press | 3 | 25 |
| dumbbell incline bench press | 3 | 25 |
| triceps curls | 3 | 25 |
| bench dips | 2 | failure |

**Day 2**

| exercise | sets | reps |
| --- | --- | --- |
| one-arm rows | 3 | 25 |
| T- bar rows | 3 | 25 |
| preacher curls | 2 | 25 |
| barbell curls | 2 | 25 |

**Day 3**

| exercise | sets | reps |
| --- | --- | --- |
| leg press | 3 | 25 |
| lunges | 3 | 25 |
| barbell military press | 3 | 25 |
| front raises | 2 | 25 |

## Program Level III
# Endurance/Fat Burning Training
Three-Day Split four days a week--Antagonistic Training

## Weeks 1 and 2

### Day 1

| exercise | sets | reps |
|---|---|---|
| barbell bench press | 3 | 20 |
| dumbbell incline bench press | 2 | 20 |
| seated cable rows | 3 | 20 |
| bent-over barbell rows | 2 | 20 |
| dips | 3 | failure |
| wide-grip lat pull downs | 2 | 20 |

### Day 2

| exercise | sets | reps |
|---|---|---|
| triceps kickbacks | 2 | 20 |
| bench dips | 2 | 20 |
| dumbbell curls | 2 | 20 |
| incline curls | 2 | 20 |
| hammer curls | 2 | 20 |
| close-grip bench press | 2 | 20 |

### Day 3

| exercise | sets | reps |
|---|---|---|
| squats | 3 | 20 |
| leg extensions | 2 | 20 |
| dumbbell military press | 3 | 20 |
| upright rows | 3 | 20 |
| lunges | 2 | 20 |
| bent-over lateral raises | 2 | 20 |

## Weeks 3 and 4

### Day 1

| exercise | sets | reps |
|---|---|---|
| dumbbell bench press | 3 | 25 |
| incline barbell bench press | 2 | 25 |
| one-arm dumbbell rows | 3 | 25 |
| T-bar rows | 2 | 25 |
| cable crossovers | 2 | 25 |
| close-grip lat pull downs | 2 | 25 |

### Day 2

| exercise | sets | reps |
|---|---|---|
| preacher curls | 2 | 25 |
| reverse curls | 2 | 25 |
| dumbbell triceps curls | 2 | 25 |
| bench dips | 2 | 25 |
| triceps pull downs | 2 | 25 |
| barbell curls | 2 | 25 |

### Day 3

| exercise | sets | reps |
|---|---|---|
| leg press | 3 | 25 |
| lunges | 3 | 25 |
| barbell Military press | 3 | 25 |
| lateral raises | 2 | 25 |
| seated calf raises | 3 | 25 |
| cable lateral raises | 2 | 25 |

## Program Level III
# Endurance/Fat Burning Training
Three-Day Split four days a week--Synergistic Training

## Weeks 1 and 2

### Day 1

| exercise | sets | reps |
|---|---|---|
| dumbbell bench press | 3 | 20 |
| incline barbell bench press | 3 | 20 |
| triceps kickbacks | 2 | 20 |
| bench dips | 2 | failure |
| close-grip bench press | 2 | 20 |
| dips | 3 | failure |

### Day 2

| exercise | sets | reps |
|---|---|---|
| seated cable rows | 3 | 20 |
| bent-over barbell rows | 3 | 20 |
| dumbbell curls | 2 | 20 |
| incline curls | 2 | 20 |
| wide-grip lat pull downs | 3 | 20 |
| hammer curls | 3 | 20 |

### Day 3

| exercise | sets | reps |
|---|---|---|
| squats | 3 | 20 |
| leg curls | 2 | 20 |
| dumbbell military press | 3 | 20 |
| upright rows | 3 | 20 |
| lunges | 2 | 20 |
| bent-over lateral raises | 2 | 20 |

## Weeks 3 and 4

### Day 1

| exercise | sets | reps |
|---|---|---|
| barbell bench press | 3 | 25 |
| incline dumbbell bench press | 3 | 25 |
| triceps curls | 3 | 25 |
| bench dips | 2 | failure |
| cable crossovers | 2 | 25 |
| dips | 3 | failure |

### Day 2

| exercise | sets | reps |
|---|---|---|
| one-arm dumbbell rows | 3 | 25 |
| T- bar rows | 3 | 25 |
| preacher curls | 2 | 25 |
| barbell curls | 2 | 25 |
| close-grip lat pull downs | 3 | 25 |
| concentration curls | 2 | 25 |

### Day 3

| exercise | sets | reps |
|---|---|---|
| leg press | 3 | 25 |
| lunges | 3 | 25 |
| barbell military press | 3 | 25 |
| lateral raises | 2 | 25 |
| seated calf raises | 3 | 25 |
| cable lateral raises | 2 | 25 |

## Program Level III
# Endurance/Fat Burning Training
Two-Day Split 4 days per week
Upper & lower body training on the same day
Antagonistic Training

## Weeks 1 and 2

### Days 1 and 3

| exercise | sets | reps |
|---|---|---|
| barbell bench press | 3 | 20 |
| dumbbell military press | 3 | 20 |
| wide-grip pull-ups | 3 | 20 |
| leg press | 3 | 20 |

### Days 2 and 4

| exercise | sets | reps |
|---|---|---|
| leg curls | 3 | 20 |
| standing calf raises | 3 | 20 |
| dumbbell curls | 2 | 20 |
| triceps curls | 2 | 20 |

## Weeks 3 and 4

### Days 1 and 3

| exercise | sets | reps |
|---|---|---|
| dumbbell bench press | 3 | 25 |
| barbell military press | 3 | 25 |
| close grip lat pull downs | 3 | 25 |
| leg curls | 2 | 25 |

### Days 2 and 4

| exercise | sets | reps |
|---|---|---|
| squats | 3 | 25 |
| seated calf raises | 2 | 25 |
| barbell curls | 2 | 25 |
| one-arm triceps extension | 2 | 25 |

## Program Level III
# Endurance/Fat Burning Training
Two-Day Split 4 days per week
Upper & lower body training on different days

## Weeks 1 and 2

### Days 1 and 3

| exercise | sets | reps |
|---|---|---|
| barbell bench press | 3 | 20,20,20 |
| barbell military press | 3 | 20,20,20 |
| bent-over dumbbell rows | 3 | 20,20,20 |
| hammer curls | 2 | 20,20 |

### Days 2 and 4

| exercise | sets | reps |
|---|---|---|
| squats | 3 | 20,20,20 |
| leg press | 3 | 20,20,20 |
| seated calf raises | 3 | 20,20,20 |
| lunges | 2 | 20,20 |

## Weeks 3 and 4

### Days 1 and 3

| exercise | sets | reps |
|---|---|---|
| dumbbell bench press | 3 | 25,25,25 |
| dumbbell military press | 3 | 25,25,25 |
| bent-over barbell rows | 3 | 25,25,25 |
| reverse dumbbell curls | 2 | 25,25 |

### Days 2 and 4

| exercise | sets | reps |
|---|---|---|
| leg press | 3 | 20,20,20 |
| lunges | 2 | 20,20,20 |
| squats | 3 | 20,20,20 |
| standing calf raises | 3 | 20,20 |

## Program Level III
# Endurance/Fat Burning Training
Two-Day Split 4 days per week
Upper & lower body training on the same day -- Synergistic Training

## Weeks 1 and 2

### Days 1 and 3

| exercise | sets | reps |
|---|---|---|
| barbell bench press | 3 | 20 |
| dumbbell incline bench press | 2 | 20 |
| standing flyes | 3 | 20 |
| leg press | 3 | 20 |

### Days 2 and 4

| exercise | sets | reps |
|---|---|---|
| wide-grip pull-ups | 2 | failure |
| hammer curls | 2 | 20 |
| leg curls | 3 | 20 |
| standing calf raises | 3 | 20 |

## Weeks 3 and 4

### Days 1 and 3

| exercise | sets | reps |
|---|---|---|
| dumbbell bench press | 3 | 25 |
| barbell incline bench press | 2 | 25 |
| upright rows | 3 | 25 |
| squats | 3 | 25 |

### Days 2 and 4

| exercise | sets | reps |
|---|---|---|
| close-grip pull-ups | 2 | failure |
| reverse curls | 2 | 25 |
| leg curls | 3 | 25 |
| seated calf raises | 2 | 25 |

## Program Level III
# Endurance/Fat Burning Training
Entire body every training day -- Rest every other day

## Weeks 1 and 2

### Day 1

| exercise | sets | reps |
|---|---|---|
| barbell bench press | 3 | 20 |
| seated cable rows | 3 | 20 |
| squats | 3 | 20 |
| dumbbell military press | 3 | 20 |
| lunges | 3 | 20 |
| front raises | 2 | 20 |
| incline flyes | 2 | 20 |
| wide-grip pull-ups | 2 | failure |

### Day 2

| exercise | sets | reps |
|---|---|---|
| dumbbell bench press | 3 | 20 |
| standing flyes | 3 | 20 |
| bent-over barbell rows | 3 | 20 |
| leg curls | 3 | 20 |
| standing calf raises | 3 | 20 |
| cable crossovers | 2 | 20 |
| barbell military press | 2 | 20 |
| close-grip pull ups | 2 | failure |

### Day 3

| exercise | sets | reps |
|---|---|---|
| bench | 3 | 20 |
| seated cable rows | 3 | 20 |
| squats | 3 | 20 |
| dumbbell military | 3 | 20 |
| lunges | 3 | 20 |
| front raises | 2 | 20 |
| incline flys | 2 | 20 |
| wide-grip pull ups | 2 | failure |

## Weeks 3 and 4

### Day 1

| exercise | sets | reps |
|---|---|---|
| barbell bench press | 3 | 25 |
| seated cable rows | 3 | 25 |
| squats | 3 | 25 |
| dumbbell military press | 3 | 25 |
| lunges | 3 | 25 |
| front raises | 2 | 25 |
| incline flyes | 2 | 25 |
| wide-grip pull-ups | 2 | failure |

### Day 2

| exercise | sets | reps |
|---|---|---|
| dumbbell bench press | 3 | 25 |
| standing flyes | 3 | 25 |
| bent-over barbell rows | 3 | 25 |
| leg curls | 3 | 25 |
| standing calf raises | 3 | 25 |
| cable crossovers | 2 | 25 |
| barbell military press | 2 | 25 |
| close-grip pull-ups | 2 | failure |

### Day 3

| exercise | sets | reps |
|---|---|---|
| barbell bench press | 3 | 25 |
| seated cable rows | 3 | 25 |
| squats | 3 | 25 |
| dumbbell military press | 3 | 25 |
| lunges | 3 | 25 |
| front raises | 2 | 25 |
| incline flyes | 2 | 25 |
| wide-grip pull-ups | 2 | failure |

# Endurance/Fat Burning Training
Three-Day Split four days a week -- Antagonistic Training

## Weeks 1 and 2

### Day 1

| exercise | sets | reps |
|---|---|---|
| barbell bench press | 3 | 20 |
| dumbbell incline bench press | 2 | 20 |
| seated cable rows | 3 | 20 |
| bent-over barbell rows | 2 | 20 |
| dips | 3 | failure |
| wide-grip lat pull downs | 2 | 20 |
| flyes | 2 | 20 |
| wide-grip pull-ups | 2 | failure |

### Day 2

| exercise | sets | reps |
|---|---|---|
| triceps kickbacks | 2 | 20 |
| bench dips | 2 | 20 |
| dumbbell curls | 2 | 20 |
| incline curls | 2 | 20 |
| hammer curls | 2 | 20 |
| close-grip bench press | 2 | 20 |
| triceps push downs | 2 | 20 |
| behind back wrist curls | 2 | 20 |

### Day 3

| exercise | sets | reps |
|---|---|---|
| squats | 3 | 20 |
| leg curls | 2 | 20 |
| dumbbell military press | 3 | 20 |
| upright rows | 3 | 20 |
| lunges | 2 | 20 |
| bent-over lateral raises | 2 | 20 |
| standing flyes | 2 | 20 |
| standing calf raises | 3 | 20 |

## Weeks 3 and 4

### Day 1

| exercise | sets | reps |
|---|---|---|
| dumbbell bench press | 3 | 25 |
| incline barbell bench press | 2 | 25 |
| one-arm dumbbell rows | 3 | 25 |
| T-bar rows | 2 | 25 |
| cable crossovers | 2 | 25 |
| close-grip lat pull downs | 2 | 25 |
| dips | 3 | failure |
| close-grip pull-ups | 2 | failure |

### Day 2

| exercise | sets | reps |
|---|---|---|
| preacher curls | 2 | 25 |
| reverse curls | 2 | 25 |
| barbell triceps curls | 2 | 25 |
| bench dips | 2 | 25 |
| triceps pull downs | 2 | 25 |
| barbell curls | 2 | 25 |
| reverse wrist curls | 2 | 25 |
| one-arm triceps extensions | 2 | 25 |

### Day 3

| exercise | sets | reps |
|---|---|---|
| leg press | 3 | 25 |
| lunges | 3 | 25 |
| barbell military press | 3 | 25 |
| lateral raises | 2 | 25 |
| seated calf raises | 3 | 25 |
| cable lateral raises | 2 | 25 |
| dumbbell shrugs | 3 | 25 |
| leg curls | 2 | 25 |

# Endurance/Fat Burning Training
Three-Day Split four days a week -- Synergistic Training

## Weeks 1 and 2

### Day 1

| exercise | sets | reps |
|---|---|---|
| barbell bench press | 3 | 10,10,10 |
| dumbbell incline bench press | 3 | 12,12,12 |
| bench dips | 3 | failure |
| dumbbells triceps curls | 3 | 15,15,15 |
| cable crossovers | 3 | 15,15,15 |
| one-arm triceps extensions | 3 | 15,15,15 |
| dips | 3 | failure |
| triceps kickbacks | 3 | 15,15,15 |

### Day 2

| exercise | sets | reps |
|---|---|---|
| wide-grip lat pull down | 3 | 10,10,10 |
| T-bar row | 3 | 12,12,12 |
| barbell curls | 3 | failure |
| concentration curls | 3 | 15,15,15 |
| seated cable rows | 3 | 15,15,15 |
| bent-over barbell rows | 3 | 15,15,15 |
| hammer curls | 3 | 12,12,12 |
| preacher curls | 3 | 15,15,15 |

### Day 3

| exercise | sets | reps |
|---|---|---|
| jump squats | 3 | 10,10,10 |
| power cleans | 3 | 12,12,12 |
| dumbbell military press | 3 | 10,10,10 |
| push press | 3 | 12,12,12 |
| leg press | 3 | 8,8,8 |
| bent-over lateral raises | 3 | 15,15,15 |
| standing flyes | 3 | 12,12,12 |
| standing calf raises | 3 | 20,20,20 |

## Weeks 3 and 4

### Day 1

| exercise | sets | reps |
|---|---|---|
| dumbbell bench press | 3 | 10,10,10 |
| incline barbell bench press | 3 | 12,12,12 |
| close-grip bench press | 3 | 12,12,12 |
| skull crushers | 3 | 15,15,15 |
| incline flyes | 3 | 15,15,15 |
| triceps push downs | 3 | 15,15,15 |
| dips | 3 | failure |
| one-arm triceps extensions | 3 | 15,15,15 |

### Day 2

| exercise | sets | reps |
|---|---|---|
| close-grip pull-ups | 3 | failure |
| seated cable rows | 3 | 10,10,10 |
| preacher curls | 3 | 15,15,15 |
| concentration curls | 3 | 15,15,15 |
| bent-over dumbbell rows | 3 | 12,12,12 |
| hammer curls | 3 | 15,15,15 |
| reverse wrist curls | 3 | 15,15,15 |
| close-grip lat pull downs | 3 | 12,12,12 |

### Day 3

| exercise | sets | reps |
|---|---|---|
| jump squats | 3 | 10,10,10 |
| box steps | 3 | 12,12,12 |
| barbell military press | 3 | 10,10,10 |
| push press | 3 | 12,12,12 |
| squats | 3 | 8,8,8 |
| upright rows | 3 | 12,12,12 |
| front raises | 3 | 15,15,15 |
| seated calf raises | 3 | 20,20,20 |

# Endurance/Fat Burning Training
Two-Day Split 4 days per week
Upper & lower body training on the same day
Antagonistic Training

## Weeks 1 and 2

### Days 1 and 3

| exercise | sets | reps |
| --- | --- | --- |
| barbell bench press | 3 | 10,10,10 |
| wide-grip pull-ups | 2 | failure |
| push press | 3 | 12,12,12 |
| leg curls | 3 | 12,12,12 |
| standing calf raises | 3 | 20,20,20 |
| dips | 2 | failure |

### Days 2 and 4

| exercise | sets | reps |
| --- | --- | --- |
| leg press | 3 | 12,12,12 |
| power cleans | 3 | 12,12,12 |
| bench dips | 2 | failure |
| preacher curls | 4 | 12,12,12,12 |
| reverse curls | 3 | 12,12,12 |
| triceps kickbacks | 4 | 12,12,12 |

## Weeks 3 and 4

### Days 1 and 3

| exercise | sets | reps |
| --- | --- | --- |
| dumbbell bench press | 3 | 12,12,12 |
| close-grip pull-ups | 3 | failure |
| push press | 3 | 12,12,12 |
| leg curls | 3 | 15,15,15 |
| standing calf raises | 3 | 20,20,20 |
| dips | 3 | failure |

### Days 2 and 4

| exercise | sets | reps |
| --- | --- | --- |
| power cleans | 3 | 10,10,10 |
| box steps | 3 | 12,12,12 |
| concentration curls | 4 | 15,15,15,15 |
| triceps curls | 4 | 15,15,15,15 |
| bench dips | 3 | failure |
| hammer curls | 3 | 12,12,12 |

## Program Level IV
# Endurance/Fat Burning Training
Two-Day Split 4 days per week
Upper & lower body training on different days

## Weeks 1 and 2

### Days 1 and 3

| exercise | sets | reps |
| --- | --- | --- |
| barbell bench press | 3 | 10,10,10 |
| push press | 3 | 12,12,12 |
| wide-grip pull-ups | 2 | failure |
| reverse curls | 3 | 15,15,15 |
| dips | 2 | failure |
| bent-over dumbbell rows | 3 | 12,12,12 |

### Days 2 and 4

| exercise | sets | reps |
| --- | --- | --- |
| jump squats | 3 | 10,10,10 |
| power cleans | 3 | 12,12,12 |
| squats | 3 | 8,8,8 |
| lunges | 3 | 10,10,10 |
| box steps | 3 | 12,12,12 |
| standing calf raises | 3 | 20,20,20 |

## Weeks 3 and 4

### Days 1 and 3

| exercise | sets | reps |
| --- | --- | --- |
| dumbbell bench press | 3 | 10,10,10 |
| push press | 3 | 12,12,12 |
| close-grip pull-ups | 3 | failure |
| hammer curls | 3 | 15,15,15 |
| cable crossovers | 3 | 10,10,10 |
| T-bar rows | 3 | 12,12,12 |

### Days 2 and 4

| exercise | sets | reps |
| --- | --- | --- |
| squats | 3 | 8,8,8 |
| lunges | 3 | 10,10,10 |
| jump squats | 3 | 10,10,10 |
| power cleans | 3 | 12,12,12 |
| box steps | 3 | 12,12,12 |
| standing calf raises | 3 | 20,20,20 |

## Program Level IV
# Endurance/Fat Burning Training
Two-Day Split 4 days per week
Upper & lower body training on the same day -- Synergistic Training

### Weeks 1 and 2

#### Days 1 and 3

| exercise | sets | reps |
|---|---|---|
| barbell bench press | 3 | 20 |
| dumbbell incline bench press | 2 | 20 |
| standing flyes | 3 | 20 |
| leg press | 3 | 20 |
| dips | 2 | failure |
| lunges | 2 | 20 |

#### Days 2 and 4

| exercise | sets | reps |
|---|---|---|
| wide-grip pull-ups | 2 | failure |
| hammer curls | 2 | 20 |
| leg curls | 3 | 20 |
| standing calf raises | 3 | 20 |
| seated rows | 3 | 20 |
| dumbbell curls | 2 | 20 |

### Weeks 3 and 4

#### Days 1 and 3

| exercise | sets | reps |
|---|---|---|
| dumbbell bench press | 3 | 25 |
| incline barbell bench press | 2 | 25 |
| upright rows | 3 | 25 |
| squats | 3 | 25 |
| leg extensions | 2 | 25 |
| bench dips | 3 | failure |

#### Days 2 and 4

| exercise | sets | reps |
|---|---|---|
| close-grip pull-ups | 2 | failure |
| reverse curls | 2 | 25 |
| leg curls | 3 | 25 |
| seated calf raises | 2 | 25 |
| one-arm dumbbell rows | 3 | 25 |
| incline dumbbell curls | 2 | 25 |

## Program Level V
# Endurance/Fat Burning Training
Two-Day Split 4 days per week
Upper & lower body training on the same day -- Antagonistic Training

### Weeks 1 and 2

#### Days 1 and 3

| exercise | sets | reps |
|---|---|---|
| barbell bench press | 3 | 20 |
| dumbbell military press | 3 | 20 |
| wide-grip pull ups | 3 | 20 |
| leg press | 3 | 20 |
| incline flyes | 2 | 20 |
| lunges | 2 | 20 |
| seated rows | 2 | 20 |
| dips | 2 | failure |

#### Days 2 and 4

| exercise | sets | reps |
|---|---|---|
| leg curls | 3 | 20 |
| standing calf raises | 3 | 20 |
| dumbbell curls | 2 | 20 |
| triceps curls | 2 | 20 |
| hammer curls | 2 | 20 |
| triceps kickbacks | 2 | 20 |
| seated calf raises | 2 | 20 |
| bench dips | 2 | failure |

### Weeks 3 and 4

#### Days 1 and 3

| exercise | sets | reps |
|---|---|---|
| dumbbell bench press | 3 | 25 |
| barbell military press | 3 | 25 |
| close-grip pull downs | 3 | 25 |
| leg curls | 2 | 25 |
| incline barbell bench press | 2 | 25 |
| leg extensions | 2 | 25 |
| dips | 3 | failure |
| close-grip pull-ups | 2 | failure |

#### Days 2 and 4

| exercise | sets | reps |
|---|---|---|
| squats | 3 | 25 |
| seated calf raises | 2 | 25 |
| barbell curls | 2 | 25 |
| one-arm triceps extension | 2 | 25 |
| reverse curls | 2 | 25 |
| bench dips | 3 | failure |
| standing calf raises | 3 | 25 |
| skull crushers | 2 | 25 |

# Endurance/Fat Burning Training
Two-Day Split 4 days per week
Upper & lower body training on different days

## Weeks 1 and 2

### Days 1 and 3

| exercise | sets | reps |
|---|---|---|
| barbell bench press | 3 | 20,20,20 |
| barbell Military press | 3 | 20,20,20 |
| bent-over dumbbell rows | 3 | 20,20,20 |
| hammer curls | 2 | 20,20 |
| dips | 2 | failure |
| wide-grip pull ups | 2 | failure |
| cable crossovers | 2 | 20,20 |
| skull crushers | 2 | 20,20 |

### Days 2 and 4

| exercise | sets | reps |
|---|---|---|
| squats | 3 | 20,20,20 |
| leg press | 3 | 20,20,20 |
| standing calf raises | 3 | 20,20,20 |
| lunges | 2 | 20,20 |
| leg extensions | 2 | 20,20 |
| leg curls | 2 | 20,20 |
| seated calf raises | 2 | 20,20 |
| dead lift | 2 | 20,20 |

## Weeks 3 and 4

### Days 1 and 3

| exercise | sets | reps |
|---|---|---|
| dumbbell bench press | 3 | 25,25,25 |
| dumbbell military press | 3 | 25,25,25 |
| bent-over barbell rows | 3 | 25,25,25 |
| reverse curls | 2 | 25,25 |
| close-grip pull ups | 3 | failure |
| dumbbell curls | 2 | 25,25 |
| incline flyes | 2 | 25,25 |
| dips | 3 | 25,25,25 |

### Days 2 and 4

| exercise | sets | reps |
|---|---|---|
| squats | 3 | 25,25,25 |
| leg extensions | 2 | 25,25 |
| leg curls | 2 | 25,25 |
| leg press | 3 | 25,25,25 |
| dead lift | 2 | 25,25 |
| lunges | 2 | 25,25 |
| standing calf raises | 3 | 25,25,25 |
| seated calf raises | 2 | 25,25 |

# Endurance/Fat Burning Training
Two-Day Split 4 days per week
Upper & lower body training on the same day
Synergistic Training

## Weeks 1 and 2

### Days 1 and 3

| exercise | sets | reps |
|---|---|---|
| barbell bench press | 3 | 20 |
| dumbbell incline bench press | 2 | 20 |
| standing flyes | 3 | 20 |
| leg press | 3 | 20 |
| dips | 2 | failure |
| lunges | 2 | 20 |
| bench dips | 2 | failure |
| dumbbell military press | 3 | 20 |

### Days 2 and 4

| exercise | sets | reps |
|---|---|---|
| wide-grip pull-ups | 2 | failure |
| hammer curls | 2 | 20 |
| leg curls | 3 | 20 |
| standing calf raises | 3 | 20 |
| seated rows | 3 | 20 |
| dumbbell curls | 2 | 20 |
| seated calf raises | 2 | 20 |
| wide-grip pull downs | 2 | 20 |

## Weeks 3 and 4

### Days 1 and 3

| exercise | sets | reps |
|---|---|---|
| dumbbell bench press | 3 | 25 |
| Incline barbell bench press | 2 | 25 |
| upright rows | 3 | 25 |
| squats | 3 | 25 |
| leg extensions | 2 | 25 |
| bench dips | 3 | failure |
| dips | 3 | failure |
| front raises | 2 | 25 |

### Days 2 and 4

| exercise | sets | reps |
|---|---|---|
| close-grip pull-ups | 2 | failure |
| reverse curls | 2 | 25 |
| leg curls | 3 | 25 |
| seated calf raises | 2 | 25 |
| one-arm dumbbell rows | 3 | 25 |
| incline dumbbell curls | 2 | 25 |
| standing calf raises | 3 | 25 |
| close-grip pull downs | 2 | 25 |

# Power/
# General Fitness
# Training

## Program Level I
# Power/General Fitness Training
Entire body every training day
Rest every other day

## Weeks 1 and 2

### Day 1

| exercise | sets | reps |
|---|---|---|
| barbell bench press | 3 | 12,12,12 |
| push press | 3 | 10,10,10 |
| wide-grip pull-ups | 2 | failure |
| power cleans | 3 | 12,12,12 |

### Day 2

| exercise | sets | reps |
|---|---|---|
| dumbbell incline bench press | 3 | 12,12,12 |
| upright rows | 3 | 10,10,10 |
| close-grip pull-ups | 2 | failure |
| leg curls | 3 | 12,12,12 |

### Day 3

| exercise | sets | reps |
|---|---|---|
| dumbbell bench press | 3 | 12,12,12 |
| push press | 3 | 10,10,10 |
| wide-grip pull-ups | 2 | failure |
| power cleans | 3 | 12,12,12 |

## Weeks 3 and 4

### Day 1

| exercise | sets | reps |
|---|---|---|
| barbell bench press | 3 | 12,12,12 |
| push press | 3 | 10,10,10 |
| wide-grip pull-ups | 2 | failure |
| power cleans | 3 | 12,12,12 |

### Day 2

| exercise | sets | reps |
|---|---|---|
| dumbbell incline bench press | 3 | 12,12,12 |
| upright rows | 3 | 10,10,10 |
| close-grip pull-ups | 2 | failure |
| leg curls | 3 | 12,12,12 |

### Day 3

| exercise | sets | reps |
|---|---|---|
| dumbbell bench press | 3 | 12,12,12 |
| push press | 3 | 10,10,10 |
| wide-grip pull-ups | 2 | failure |
| power cleans | 3 | 12,12,12 |

## Program Level II
# Power/General Fitness Training
Entire body every training day
Rest every other day

## Weeks 1 and 2

### Day 1

| exercise | sets | reps |
|---|---|---|
| barbell bench press | 3 | 12,12,12 |
| push press | 3 | 10,10,10 |
| wide-grip pull-ups | 2 | failure |
| power cleans | 3 | 12,12,12 |
| jump squats | 3 | 10,10,10 |
| standing flyes | 3 | 15,15,15 |

### Day 2

| exercise | sets | reps |
|---|---|---|
| dumbbell incline bench press | 3 | 12,12,12 |
| upright rows | 3 | 10,10,10 |
| close-grip pull-ups | 2 | failure |
| leg curls | 3 | 12,12,12 |
| barbell military press | 3 | 10,10,10 |
| standing calf raises | 3 | 20,20,20 |

### Day 3

| exercise | sets | reps |
|---|---|---|
| dumbbell bench press | 3 | 12,12,12 |
| push press | 3 | 10,10,10 |
| wide-grip pull-ups | 2 | failure |
| power cleans | 3 | 12,12,12 |
| box steps | 3 | 10,10,10 |
| standing flyes | 3 | 15,15,15 |

## Weeks 3 and 4

### Day 1

| exercise | sets | reps |
|---|---|---|
| barbell bench press | 3 | 12,12,12 |
| push press | 3 | 10,10,10 |
| wide-grip pull-ups | 2 | failure |
| power cleans | 3 | 12,12,12 |
| jump squats | 3 | 10,10,10 |
| standing flyes | 3 | 15,15,15 |

### Day 2

| exercise | sets | reps |
|---|---|---|
| dumbbell incline bench press | 3 | 12,12,12 |
| upright rows | 3 | 10,10,10 |
| close-grip pull-ups | 2 | failure |
| leg curls | 3 | 12,12,12 |
| barbell military press | 3 | 10,10,10 |
| standing calf raises | 3 | 20,20,20 |

### Day 3

| exercise | sets | reps |
|---|---|---|
| dumbbell bench press | 3 | 12,12,12 |
| push press | 3 | 10,10,10 |
| wide-grip pull-ups | 2 | failure |
| power cleans | 3 | 12,12,12 |
| box steps | 3 | 10,10,10 |
| standing flyes | 3 | 15,15,15 |

## Program Level II
# Power/General Fitness Training
Three-Day Split four days a week
Antagonistic Training

### Weeks 1 and 2

| Day 1 | | | | Day 2 | | | | Day 3 | | |
|---|---|---|---|---|---|---|---|---|---|---|
| exercise | sets | reps | | exercise | sets | reps | | exercise | sets | reps |
| barbell bench press | 3 | 10,10,10 | | bench dips | 3 | failure | | jump squats | 3 | 10,10,10 |
| incline dumbbell bench press | 3 | 12,12,12 | | dumbbell triceps curls | 3 | 15,15,15 | | power cleans | 3 | 12,12,12 |
| wide-grip pull-ups | 3 | failure | | barbell curls | 3 | 15,15,15 | | dumbbell military press | 3 | 10,10,10 |
| T-bar rows | 3 | 10,10,10 | | Incline dumbbell curls | 3 | 15,15,15 | | push press | 3 | 12,12,12 |

### Weeks 3 and 4

| Day 1 | | | | Day 2 | | | | Day 3 | | |
|---|---|---|---|---|---|---|---|---|---|---|
| exercise | sets | reps | | exercise | sets | reps | | exercise | sets | reps |
| dumbbell bench press | 3 | 10,10,10 | | close-grip bench press | 3 | 15,15,15 | | jump squats | 3 | 10,10,10 |
| incline barbell bench press | 3 | 12,12,12 | | skull crushers | 3 | 15,15,15 | | box steps | 3 | 12,12,12 |
| close-grip pull-ups | 3 | failure | | preacher curls | 3 | 15,15,15 | | barbell military press | 3 | 10,10,10 |
| seated cable rows | 3 | 10,10,10 | | concentration curls | 3 | 15,15,15 | | push press | 3 | 12,12,12 |

## Program Level II
# Power/General Fitness Training
Three-Day Split four days a week
Synergistic Training

### Weeks 1 and 2

| Day 1 | | | | Day 2 | | | | Day 3 | | |
|---|---|---|---|---|---|---|---|---|---|---|
| exercise | sets | reps | | exercise | sets | reps | | exercise | sets | reps |
| barbell bench press | 3 | 10,10,10 | | wide-grip pull-ups | 3 | failure | | jump squats | 3 | 10,10,10 |
| incline dumbbell bench press | 3 | 12,12,12 | | T-bar rows | 3 | 10,10,10 | | power cleans | 3 | 12,12,12 |
| bench dips | 3 | failure | | barbell curls | 3 | 15,15,15 | | dumbbell military press | 3 | 10,10,10 |
| triceps curls | 3 | 15,15,15 | | incline dumbbell curls | 3 | 15,15,15 | | push press | 3 | 12,12,12 |

### Weeks 3 and 4

| Day 1 | | | | Day 2 | | | | Day 3 | | |
|---|---|---|---|---|---|---|---|---|---|---|
| exercise | sets | reps | | exercise | sets | reps | | exercise | sets | reps |
| dumbbell bench press | 3 | 10,10,10 | | close-grip pull-ups | 3 | failure | | jump squats | 3 | 10,10,10 |
| incline barbell bench press | 3 | 12,12,12 | | seated cable rows | 3 | 10,10,10 | | box steps | 3 | 12,12,12 |
| close-grip bench press | 3 | 12,12,12 | | preacher curls | 3 | 15,15,15 | | barbell military press | 3 | 10,10,10 |
| skull crushers | 3 | 15,15,15 | | concentration curls | 3 | 15,15,15 | | push press | 3 | 12,12,12 |

# Power/General Fitness Training
Three-Day Split four days a week
Antagonistic Training

## Weeks 1 and 2

### Day 1

| exercise | sets | reps |
|---|---|---|
| barbell bench press | 3 | 10,10,10 |
| dumbbell incline bench press | 3 | 12,12,12 |
| wide-grip pull-ups | 3 | failure |
| T-bar rows | 3 | 10,10,10 |
| cable crossovers | 3 | 15,15,15 |
| one-arm dumbbell rows | 3 | 12,12,12 |

### Day 2

| exercise | sets | reps |
|---|---|---|
| bench dips | 3 | failure |
| barbell triceps curls | 3 | 15,15,15 |
| barbell curls | 3 | 15,15,15 |
| incline dumbbell curls | 3 | 15,15,15 |
| reverse curls | 3 | 15,15,15 |
| one-arm triceps extensions | 3 | 15,15,15 |

### Day 3

| exercise | sets | reps |
|---|---|---|
| jump squats | 3 | 10,10,10 |
| power cleans | 3 | 12,12,12 |
| dumbbell military press | 3 | 10,10,10 |
| push press | 3 | 12,12,12 |
| leg press | 3 | 8,8,8 |
| bent-over lateral raises | 3 | 15,15,15 |

## Weeks 3 and 4

### Day 1

| exercise | sets | reps |
|---|---|---|
| dumbbell bench press | 3 | 10,10,10 |
| incline barbell bench press | 3 | 12,12,12 |
| close-grip pull-ups | 3 | failure |
| seated cable rows | 3 | 10,10,10 |
| flyes | 3 | 15,15,15 |
| bent-over barbell rows | 3 | 12,12,12 |

### Day 2

| exercise | sets | reps |
|---|---|---|
| close-grip bench press | 3 | 15,15,15 |
| skull crushers | 3 | 15,15,15 |
| preacher curls | 3 | 15,15,15 |
| concentration curls | 3 | 15,15,15 |
| hammer curls | 3 | 15,15,15 |
| triceps push downs | 3 | 15,15,15 |

### Day 3

| exercise | sets | reps |
|---|---|---|
| jump squats | 3 | 10,10,10 |
| box steps | 3 | 12,12,12 |
| barbell military press | 3 | 10,10,10 |
| push press | 3 | 12,12,12 |
| squats | 3 | 8,8,8 |
| upright rows | 3 | 12,12,12 |

# Power/General Fitness Training
Three-Day Split four days a week
Synergistic Training

## Weeks 1 and 2

### Day 1

| exercise | sets | reps |
|---|---|---|
| barbell bench press | 3 | 10,10,10 |
| incline dumbbell bench press | 3 | 12,12,12 |
| bench dips | 3 | failure |
| dumbbell triceps curls | 3 | 15,15,15 |
| cable crossovers | 3 | 15,15,15 |
| one-arm triceps extensions | 3 | 15,15,15 |

### Day 2

| exercise | sets | reps |
|---|---|---|
| wide-grip pull-ups | 3 | failure |
| T-bar rows | 3 | 10,10,10 |
| barbell curls | 3 | 15,15,15 |
| incline dumbbell curls | 3 | 15,15,15 |
| one-arm dumbbell rows | 3 | 12,12,12 |
| reverse curls | 3 | 15,15,15 |

### Day 3

| exercise | sets | reps |
|---|---|---|
| jump squats | 3 | 10,10,10 |
| power cleans | 3 | 12,12,12 |
| dumbbell military press | 3 | 10,10,10 |
| push press | 3 | 12,12,12 |
| leg press | 3 | 8,8,8 |
| bent-over lateral raises | 3 | 15,15,15 |

## Weeks 3 and 4

### Day 1

| exercise | sets | reps |
|---|---|---|
| dumbbell bench press | 3 | 10,10,10 |
| incline barbell bench press | 3 | 12,12,12 |
| close-grip bench press | 3 | 12,12,12 |
| skull crushers | 3 | 15,15,15 |
| incline flyes | 3 | 15,15,15 |
| triceps push downs | 3 | 15,15,15 |

### Day 2

| exercise | sets | reps |
|---|---|---|
| close-grip pull-ups | 3 | failure |
| seated cable rows | 3 | 10,10,10 |
| preacher curls | 3 | 15,15,15 |
| concentration curls | 3 | 15,15,15 |
| bent-over dumbbell rows | 3 | 12,12,12 |
| hammer curls | 3 | 15,15,15 |

### Day 3

| exercise | sets | reps |
|---|---|---|
| jump squats | 3 | 10,10,10 |
| box steps | 3 | 12,12,12 |
| barbell military press | 3 | 10,10,10 |
| push press | 3 | 12,12,12 |
| squats | 3 | 8,8,8 |
| upright rows | 3 | 12,12,12 |

## Program Level III
# Power/General Fitness Training
Two-Day Split 4 days per week
Upper & lower body training on the same day -- Antagonistic Training

## Weeks 1 and 2

### Days 1 and 3

| exercise | sets | reps |
|---|---|---|
| squats | 5 | 10,8,6,4,2 |
| dead lift | 5 | 10,8,6,4,2 |
| preacher curls | 4 | 12,10,8,6 |
| triceps push downs | 4 | 12,10,8,6 |

### Days 2 and 4

| exercise | sets | reps |
|---|---|---|
| calf raises | 3 | 20,20,20 |
| power cleans | 3 | 12,12,12 |
| bench dips | 2 | failure |
| preacher curls | 4 | 12,12,12,12 |

## Weeks 3 and 4

### Days 1 and 3

| exercise | sets | reps |
|---|---|---|
| dumbbell bench press | 3 | 12,12,12 |
| close-grip pull-ups | 3 | failure |
| push press | 3 | 12,12,12 |
| leg curls | 3 | 15,15,15 |

### Days 2 and 4

| exercise | sets | reps |
|---|---|---|
| power cleans | 3 | 10,10,10 |
| box steps | 3 | 12,12,12 |
| concentration curls | 4 | 15,15,15,15 |
| triceps curls | 4 | 15,15,15,15 |

## Program Level III
# Power/General Fitness Training
Two-Day Split 4 days per week
Upper & lower body training on different days

## Weeks 1 and 2

### Days 1 and 3

| exercise | sets | reps |
|---|---|---|
| barbell bench press | 3 | 10,10,10 |
| push press | 3 | 12,12,12 |
| wide-grip pull-ups | 2 | failure |
| reverse curls | 3 | 15,15,15 |

### Days 2 and 4

| exercise | sets | reps |
|---|---|---|
| jump squats | 3 | 10,10,10 |
| cleans | 3 | 12,12,12 |
| lunges | 3 | 10,10,10 |
| standing calf raises | 3 | 20,20,20 |

## Weeks 3 and 4

### Days 1 and 3

| exercise | sets | reps |
|---|---|---|
| dumbbell bench press | 3 | 10,10,10 |
| push press | 3 | 12,12,12 |
| close-grip pull-ups | 3 | failure |
| hammer curls | 3 | 15,15,15 |

### Days 2 and 4

| exercise | sets | reps |
|---|---|---|
| lunges | 3 | 10,10,10 |
| jump squats | 3 | 10,10,10 |
| power cleans | 3 | 12,12,12 |
| standing calf raises | 3 | 20,20,20 |

## Program Level III
# Power/General Fitness Training
Two-Day Split 4 days per week
Upper & lower body training on the same day -- Synergistic Training

### Weeks 1 and 2

#### Days 1 and 3

| exercise | sets | reps |
|---|---|---|
| dumbbell bench press | 3 | 10,10,10 |
| push press | 3 | 12,12,12 |
| dumbbell incline bench press | 3 | 12,12,12 |
| leg curls | 3 | 12,12,12 |

#### Days 2 and 4

| exercise | sets | reps |
|---|---|---|
| wide-grip pull-ups | 2 | failure |
| reverse curls | 3 | 12,12,12 |
| squats | 4 | 10,10,10 |
| box steps | 3 | 12,12,12 |

### Weeks 3 and 4

#### Days 1 and 3

| exercise | sets | reps |
|---|---|---|
| barbell bench press | 3 | 12,12,12 |
| push press | 3 | 12,12,12 |
| incline barbell bench press | 3 | 12,12,12 |
| standing calf raises | 3 | 20,20,20 |

#### Days 2 and 4

| exercise | sets | reps |
|---|---|---|
| close-grip pull-ups | 3 | failure |
| hammer curls | 4 | 12,12,12,12 |
| jump squats | 3 | 10,10,10 |
| power cleans | 3 | 12,12,12 |

## Program Level III
# Power/General Fitness Training
Entire body every training day -- Rest every other day

### Weeks 1 and 2

#### Day 1

| exercise | sets | reps |
|---|---|---|
| barbell bench press | 3 | 12,12,12 |
| push press | 3 | 10,10,10 |
| wide-grip pull-ups | 2 | failure |
| power cleans | 3 | 12,12,12 |
| jump squats | 3 | 10,10,10 |
| standing flyes | 3 | 15,15,15 |
| T-bar rows | 3 | 12,12,12 |
| cable crossovers | 3 | 10,10,10 |

#### Day 2

| exercise | sets | reps |
|---|---|---|
| dumbbell incline bench press | 3 | 12,12,12 |
| upright rows | 3 | 10,10,10 |
| close-grip pull-ups | 2 | failure |
| leg curls | 3 | 12,12,12 |
| barbell military press | 3 | 10,10,10 |
| standing calf raises | 3 | 20,20,20 |
| seated cable rows | 3 | 12,12,12 |
| incline flyes | 3 | 10,10,10 |

#### Day 3

| exercise | sets | reps |
|---|---|---|
| dumbbell bench press | 3 | 12,12,12 |
| push press | 3 | 10,10,10 |
| wide-grip pull-ups | 2 | failure |
| power cleans | 3 | 12,12,12 |
| box steps | 3 | 10,10,10 |
| standing flyes | 3 | 15,15,15 |
| T-bar rows | 3 | 12,12,12 |
| cable crossovers | 3 | 10,10,10 |

### Weeks 3 and 4

#### Day 1

| exercise | sets | reps |
|---|---|---|
| barbell bench press | 3 | 12,12,12 |
| push press | 3 | 10,10,10 |
| wide-grip pull-ups | 2 | failure |
| power cleans | 3 | 12,12,12 |
| jump squats | 3 | 10,10,10 |
| standing flyes | 3 | 15,15,15 |
| T-bar rows | 3 | 12,12,12 |
| cable crossovers | 3 | 10,10,10 |

#### Day 2

| exercise | sets | reps |
|---|---|---|
| dumbbell incline bench press | 3 | 12,12,12 |
| upright rows | 3 | 10,10,10 |
| close-grip pull-ups | 2 | failure |
| leg curls | 3 | 12,12,12 |
| barbell military press | 3 | 10,10,10 |
| standing calf raises | 3 | 20,20,20 |
| seated cable rows | 3 | 12,12,12 |
| incline flyes | 3 | 10,10,10 |

#### Day 3

| exercise | sets | reps |
|---|---|---|
| dumbbell bench press | 3 | 12,12,12 |
| push press | 3 | 10,10,10 |
| wide-grip pull-ups | 2 | failure |
| power cleans | 3 | 12,12,12 |
| box steps | 3 | 10,10,10 |
| standing flyes | 3 | 15,15,15 |
| T-bar rows | 3 | 12,12,12 |
| cable crossovers | 3 | 10,10,10 |

## Program Level IV
# Power/General Fitness Training
Three-Day Split four days a week -- Antagonistic Training

## Weeks 1 and 2

### Day 1

| exercise | sets | reps |
|---|---|---|
| barbell bench press | 3 | 10,10,10 |
| incline dumbbell bench press | 3 | 12,12,12 |
| wide-grip pull-ups | 3 | failure |
| T-bar rows | 3 | 10,10,10 |
| cable crossovers | 3 | 15,15,15 |
| one-arm dumbbell rows | 3 | 12,12,12 |
| dips | 3 | failure |
| behind the neck pull downs | 3 | 12,12,12 |

### Day 2

| exercise | sets | reps |
|---|---|---|
| bench dips | 3 | failure |
| dumbbell triceps curls | 3 | 15,15,15 |
| barbell curls | 3 | 15,15,15 |
| incline dumbbell curls | 3 | 15,15,15 |
| reverse curls | 3 | 15,15,15 |
| one-arm triceps extensions | 3 | 15,15,15 |
| behind back wrist curls | 3 | 15,15,15 |
| triceps kickbacks | 3 | 15,15,15 |

### Day 3

| exercise | sets | reps |
|---|---|---|
| jump squats | 3 | 10,10,10 |
| power cleans | 3 | 12,12,12 |
| dumbbell military press | 3 | 10,10,10 |
| push press | 3 | 12,12,12 |
| leg press | 3 | 8,8,8 |
| bent-over lateral raises | 3 | 15,15,15 |
| standing flyes | 3 | 12,12,12 |
| standing calf raises | 3 | 20,20,20 |

## Weeks 3 and 4

### Day 1

| exercise | sets | reps |
|---|---|---|
| jump squats | 3 | 10,10,10 |
| power cleans | 3 | 12,12,12 |
| dumbbell military press | 3 | 10,10,10 |
| push press | 3 | 12,12,12 |
| leg press | 3 | 8,8,8 |
| bent-over lateral raises | 3 | 15,15,15 |
| standing flyes | 3 | 12,12,12 |
| standing calf raises | 3 | 20,20,20 |

### Day 2

| exercise | sets | reps |
|---|---|---|
| close-grip bench press | 3 | 15,15,15 |
| skull crushers | 3 | 15,15,15 |
| preacher curls | 3 | 15,15,15 |
| concentration curls | 3 | 15,15,15 |
| hammer curls | 3 | 15,15,15 |
| triceps push downs | 3 | 15,15,15 |
| reverse wrist curls | 3 | 15,15,15 |
| barbell triceps curls | 3 | 15,15,15 |

### Day 3

| exercise | sets | reps |
|---|---|---|
| jump squats | 3 | 10,10,10 |
| box steps | 3 | 12,12,12 |
| barbell military press | 3 | 10,10,10 |
| push press | 3 | 12,12,12 |
| squats | 3 | 8,8,8 |
| upright rows | 3 | 12,12,12 |
| front raises | 3 | 15,15,15 |
| seated calf raises | 3 | 20,20,20 |

## Program Level IV
# Power/General Fitness Training
Three-Day Split four days a week -- Synergistic Training

## Weeks 1 and 2

### Day 1

| exercise | sets | reps |
|---|---|---|
| barbell bench press | 3 | 10,10,10 |
| dumbbell incline bench press | 3 | 12,12,12 |
| bench dips | 3 | failure |
| dumbbells triceps curls | 3 | 15,15,15 |
| cable crossovers | 3 | 15,15,15 |
| one-arm triceps extensions | 3 | 15,15,15 |
| dips | 3 | failure |
| triceps kickbacks | 3 | 15,15,15 |

### Day 2

| exercise | sets | reps |
|---|---|---|
| wide-grip lat pull down | 3 | 10,10,10 |
| T-bar row | 3 | 12,12,12 |
| barbell curls | 3 | failure |
| concentration curls | 3 | 15,15,15 |
| seated cable rows | 3 | 15,15,15 |
| bent-over barbell rows | 3 | 15,15,15 |
| hammer curls | 3 | 12,12,12 |
| preacher curls | 3 | 15,15,15 |

### Day 3

| exercise | sets | reps |
|---|---|---|
| jump squats | 3 | 10,10,10 |
| power cleans | 3 | 12,12,12 |
| dumbbell military press | 3 | 10,10,10 |
| push press | 3 | 12,12,12 |
| leg press | 3 | 8,8,8 |
| bent-over lateral raises | 3 | 15,15,15 |
| standing flyes | 3 | 12,12,12 |
| standing calf raises | 3 | 20,20,20 |

## Weeks 3 and 4

### Day 1

| exercise | sets | reps |
|---|---|---|
| dumbbell bench press | 3 | 10,10,10 |
| incline barbell bench press | 3 | 12,12,12 |
| close-grip bench press | 3 | 12,12,12 |
| skull crushers | 3 | 15,15,15 |
| incline flyes | 3 | 15,15,15 |
| triceps push downs | 3 | 15,15,15 |
| dips | 3 | failure |
| one-arm triceps extensions | 3 | 15,15,15 |

### Day 2

| exercise | sets | reps |
|---|---|---|
| close-grip pull-ups | 3 | failure |
| seated cable rows | 3 | 10,10,10 |
| preacher curls | 3 | 15,15,15 |
| concentration curls | 3 | 15,15,15 |
| bent-over dumbbell rows | 3 | 12,12,12 |
| hammer curls | 3 | 15,15,15 |
| reverse wrist curls | 3 | 15,15,15 |
| close-grip lat pull downs | 3 | 12,12,12 |

### Day 3

| exercise | sets | reps |
|---|---|---|
| jump squats | 3 | 10,10,10 |
| box steps | 3 | 12,12,12 |
| barbell military press | 3 | 10,10,10 |
| push press | 3 | 12,12,12 |
| squats | 3 | 8,8,8 |
| upright rows | 3 | 12,12,12 |
| front raises | 3 | 15,15,15 |
| seated calf raises | 3 | 20,20,20 |

## Program Level IV
# Power/General Fitness Training
Two-Day Split 4 days per week
Upper & lower body training on the same day -- Antagonistic Training

## Weeks 1 and 2

**Days 1 and 3**

| exercise | sets | reps |
|---|---|---|
| barbell bench press | 3 | 10,10,10 |
| wide-grip pull-ups | 2 | failure |
| push press | 3 | 12,12,12 |
| leg curls | 3 | 12,12,12 |
| standing calf raises | 3 | 20,20,20 |
| dips | 2 | failure |

**Days 2 and 4**

| exercise | sets | reps |
|---|---|---|
| leg press | 3 | 12,12,12 |
| power cleans | 3 | 12,12,12 |
| bench dips | 2 | failure |
| preacher curls | 4 | 12,12,12,12 |
| reverse curls | 3 | 12,12,12 |
| triceps kickbacks | 4 | 12,12,12 |

## Weeks 3 and 4

**Days 1 and 3**

| exercise | sets | reps |
|---|---|---|
| dumbbell bench press | 3 | 12,12,12 |
| close-grip pull-ups | 3 | failure |
| push press | 3 | 12,12,12 |
| leg curls | 3 | 15,15,15 |
| standing calf raises | 3 | 20,20,20 |
| dips | 3 | failure |

**Days 2 and 4**

| exercise | sets | reps |
|---|---|---|
| power cleans | 3 | 10,10,10 |
| box steps | 3 | 12,12,12 |
| concentration curls | 4 | 15,15,15,15 |
| triceps curls | 4 | 15,15,15,15 |
| bench dips | 3 | failure |
| hammer curls | 3 | 12,12,12 |

## Program Level IV
# Power/General Fitness Training
Two-Day Split 4 days per week
Upper & lower body training on different days

## Weeks 1 and 2

**Days 1 and 3**

| exercise | sets | reps |
|---|---|---|
| barbell bench press | 3 | 10,10,10 |
| push press | 3 | 12,12,12 |
| wide-grip pull-ups | 2 | failure |
| reverse curls | 3 | 15,15,15 |
| dips | 2 | failure |
| bent-over dumbbell rows | 3 | 12,12,12 |

**Days 2 and 4**

| exercise | sets | reps |
|---|---|---|
| jump squats | 3 | 10,10,10 |
| power cleans | 3 | 12,12,12 |
| squats | 3 | 8,8,8 |
| lunges | 3 | 10,10,10 |
| box steps | 3 | 12,12,12 |
| standing calf raises | 3 | 20,20,20 |

## Weeks 3 and 4

**Days 1 and 3**

| exercise | sets | reps |
|---|---|---|
| dumbbell bench press | 3 | 10,10,10 |
| push press | 3 | 12,12,12 |
| close-grip pull-ups | 3 | failure |
| hammer curls | 3 | 15,15,15 |
| cable crossovers | 3 | 10,10,10 |
| T-bar rows | 3 | 12,12,12 |

**Days 2 and 4**

| exercise | sets | reps |
|---|---|---|
| squats | 3 | 8,8,8 |
| lunges | 3 | 10,10,10 |
| jump squats | 3 | 10,10,10 |
| power cleans | 3 | 12,12,12 |
| box steps | 3 | 12,12,12 |
| standing calf raises | 3 | 20,20,20 |

### Program Level IV
# Power/General Fitness Training
Two-Day Split 4 days per week
Upper & lower body training on the same day -- Synergistic Training

## Weeks 1 and 2

**Days 1 and 3**

| exercise | sets | reps |
|---|---|---|
| dumbbell bench press | 3 | 10,10,10 |
| push press | 3 | 12,12,12 |
| dumbbell incline bench press | 3 | 12,12,12 |
| leg curls | 3 | 12,12,12 |
| dips | 2 | failure |
| standing calf raises | 3 | 20,20,20 |

**Days 2 and 4**

| exercise | sets | reps |
|---|---|---|
| wide-grip pull-ups | 2 | failure |
| reverse curls | 3 | 12,12,12 |
| squats | 4 | 10,10,10 |
| box steps | 3 | 12,12,12 |
| T-bar rows | 3 | 12,12,12 |
| power cleans | 3 | 10,10,10 |

## Weeks 3 and 4

**Days 1 and 3**

| exercise | sets | reps |
|---|---|---|
| barbell bench press | 3 | 12,12,12 |
| push press | 3 | 12,12,12 |
| incline barbell bench press | 3 | 12,12,12 |
| standing calf raises | 3 | 20,20,20 |
| leg curls | 4 | 10,10,10 |
| bench dips | 3 | failure |

**Days 2 and 4**

| exercise | sets | reps |
|---|---|---|
| close-grip pull-ups | 3 | failure |
| hammer curls | 4 | 12,12,12,12 |
| jump squats | 3 | 10,10,10 |
| power cleans | 3 | 12,12,12 |
| box steps | 3 | 12,12,12 |
| one-arm dumbbell rows | 3 | 12,12,12 |

### Program Level V
# Power/General Fitness Training
Two-Day Split 4 days per week
Upper & lower body training on the same day -- Antagonistic Training

## Weeks 1 and 2

**Days 1 and 3**

| exercise | sets | reps |
|---|---|---|
| barbell bench press | 3 | 10,10,10 |
| wide-grip pull-ups | 2 | failure |
| push press | 3 | 12,12,12 |
| leg curls | 3 | 12,12,12 |
| standing calf raises | 3 | 20,20,20 |
| dips | 2 | failure |
| one-arm dumbbell rows | 3 | 12,12,12 |
| barbell military press | 3 | 10,10,10 |

**Days 2 and 4**

| exercise | sets | reps |
|---|---|---|
| leg press | 3 | 12,12,12 |
| power cleans | 3 | 12,12,12 |
| bench dips | 2 | failure |
| preacher curls | 4 | 12,12,12,12 |
| reverse curls | 3 | 12,12,12 |
| triceps kickbacks | 4 | 12,12,12 |
| leg extension | 3 | 15,15,15 |
| close-grip bench press | 3 | 10,10,10 |

## Weeks 3 and 4

**Days 1 and 3**

| exercise | sets | reps |
|---|---|---|
| dumbbell bench press | 3 | 12,12,12 |
| close-grip pull-ups | 3 | failure |
| push press | 3 | 12,12,12 |
| leg curls | 3 | 15,15,15 |
| standing calf raises | 3 | 20,20,20 |
| dips | 3 | failure |
| cable crossovers | 3 | 10,10,10 |
| bent-over lateral raises | 3 | 15,15,15 |

**Days 2 and 4**

| exercise | sets | reps |
|---|---|---|
| power cleans | 3 | 10,10,10 |
| box steps | 3 | 12,12,12 |
| concentration curls | 4 | 15,15,15,15 |
| triceps curls | 4 | 15,15,15,15 |
| bench dips | 3 | failure |
| hammer curls | 3 | 12,12,12 |
| jump squats | 3 | 12,12,12 |
| one-arm triceps extensions | 3 | 12,12,12 |

# Power/General Fitness Training
Two-Day Split 4 days per week
Upper & lower body training on different days

## Weeks 1 and 2

### Days 1 and 3

| exercise | sets | reps |
| --- | --- | --- |
| barbell bench press | 3 | 10,10,10 |
| push press | 3 | 12,12,12 |
| wide-grip pull-ups | 2 | failure |
| reverse curls | 3 | 15,15,15 |
| dips | 2 | failure |
| bent-over dumbbell rows | 3 | 12,12,12 |
| incline flyes | 3 | 12,12,12 |
| triceps push downs | 3 | 15,15,15 |

### Days 2 and 4

| exercise | sets | reps |
| --- | --- | --- |
| jump squats | 3 | 10,10,10 |
| power cleans | 3 | 12,12,12 |
| squats | 3 | 8,8,8 |
| lunges | 3 | 10,10,10 |
| box steps | 3 | 12,12,12 |
| leg curls | 3 | 12,12,12 |
| leg extensions | 3 | 12,12,12 |
| standing calf raises | 3 | 20,20,20 |

## Weeks 3 and 4

### Days 1 and 3

| exercise | sets | reps |
| --- | --- | --- |
| dumbbell bench press | 3 | 10,10,10 |
| push press | 3 | 12,12,12 |
| close-grip pull-ups | 3 | failure |
| hammer curls | 3 | 15,15,15 |
| cable crossovers | 3 | 10,10,10 |
| T-bar rows | 3 | 12,12,12 |
| incline bench press | 3 | 12,12,12 |
| bench dips | 3 | 15,15,15 |

### Days 2 and 4

| exercise | sets | reps |
| --- | --- | --- |
| squats | 3 | 8,8,8 |
| box steps | 3 | 12,12,12 |
| power cleans | 3 | 12,12,12 |
| jump squats | 3 | 10,10,10 |
| lunges | 3 | 10,10,10 |
| leg curls | 3 | 12,12,12 |
| leg extensions | 3 | 12,12,12 |
| standing calf raises | 3 | 20,20,20 |

## Program Level V
# Power/General Fitness Training
Two-Day Split 4 days per week
Upper & lower body training on the same day

## Weeks 1 and 2

### Days 1 and 3

| exercise | sets | reps |
|---|---|---|
| dumbbell bench press | 3 | 10,10,10 |
| push press | 3 | 12,12,12 |
| dumbbell incline bench press | 3 | 12,12,12 |
| leg curls | 3 | 12,12,12 |
| dips | 2 | failure |
| standing calf raises | 3 | 20,20,20 |
| bench dips | 2 | failure |
| bent-over lateral raises | 3 | 15,15,15 |

### Days 2 and 4

| exercise | sets | reps |
|---|---|---|
| dumbbell bench press | 3 | 10,10,10 |
| push press | 3 | 12,12,12 |
| dumbbell incline bench press | 3 | 12,12,12 |
| leg curls | 3 | 12,12,12 |
| dips | 2 | failure |
| standing calf raises | 3 | 20,20,20 |
| behind the neck pull downs | 3 | 12,12,12 |
| concentration curls | 4 | 15,15,15,15 |

## Weeks 3 and 4

### Days 1 and 3

| exercise | sets | reps |
|---|---|---|
| barbell bench press | 3 | 12,12,12 |
| push press | 3 | 12,12,12 |
| incline barbell bench press | 3 | 12,12,12 |
| standing calf raises | 3 | 20,20,20 |
| leg curls | 4 | 10,10,10 |
| bench dips | 3 | failure |
| dips | 3 | failure |
| upright rows | 3 | 12,12,12 |

### Days 2 and 4

| exercise | sets | reps |
|---|---|---|
| close-grip pull-ups | 3 | failure |
| hammer curls | 4 | 12,12,12,12 |
| jump squats | 3 | 10,10,10 |
| power cleans | 3 | 12,12,12 |
| box steps | 3 | 12,12,12 |
| one-arm dumbbell rows | 3 | 12,12,12 |
| T-bar rows | 3 | 10,10,10 |
| dumbbell curls | 3 | 12,12,12 |

# Strength
# Training

Program Level I

# Strength Training
Entire body every training day
Rest every other day

## Weeks 1 and 2

### Day 1

| exercise | sets | reps |
| --- | --- | --- |
| barbell bench press | 5 | 8,6,4,2,1 |
| barbell military press | 5 | 8,6,4,2,1 |
| wide-grip lat pull downs | 4 | 8,8,8,8 |
| squats | 5 | 10,8,6,4,2 |

### Day 2

| exercise | sets | reps |
| --- | --- | --- |
| incline barbell bench press | 5 | 8,6,4,2,1 |
| barbell military press | 5 | 8,6,4,2,1 |
| close-grip lat pull downs | 4 | 8,8,8,8 |
| leg press | 5 | 10,8,6,4,2 |

### Day 3

| exercise | sets | reps |
| --- | --- | --- |
| barbell bench press | 5 | 8,6,4,2,1 |
| barbell military press | 5 | 8,6,4,2,1 |
| wide-grip lat pull downs | 4 | 8,8,8,8 |
| squats | 5 | 10,8,6,4,2 |

## Weeks 3 and 4

### Day 1

| exercise | sets | reps |
| --- | --- | --- |
| barbell bench press | 5 | 8,6,4,2,1 |
| barbell military press | 5 | 8,6,4,2,1 |
| T-bar rows | 4 | 8,8,8,8 |
| leg press | 5 | 10,8,6,4,2 |

### Day 2

| exercise | sets | reps |
| --- | --- | --- |
| incline barbell bench press | 5 | 8,6,4,2,1 |
| barbell military press | 5 | 8,6,4,2,1 |
| seated cable rows | 4 | 8,8,8,8 |
| squats | 5 | 10,8,6,4,2 |

### Day 3

| exercise | sets | reps |
| --- | --- | --- |
| barbell bench press | 5 | 8,6,4,2,1 |
| barbell military press | 5 | 8,6,4,2,1 |
| bent-over barbell rows | 4 | 8,8,8,8 |
| leg press | 5 | 10,8,6,4,2 |

Program Level II

# Strength Training
Three-Day Split four days a week
Antagonistic Training

## Weeks 1 and 2

### Day 1

| exercise | sets | reps |
| --- | --- | --- |
| barbell bench press | 5 | 8,6,4,2,1 |
| incline barbell bench press | 5 | 8,6,4,2,1 |
| wide-grip lat pull downs | 4 | 8,8,8,8 |
| seated cable rows | 4 | 8,8,8,8 |

### Day 2

| exercise | sets | reps |
| --- | --- | --- |
| squats | 5 | 10,8,6,4,2 |
| leg press | 5 | 10,8,6,4,2 |
| barbell military press | 5 | 8,6,4,2,1 |
| upright rows | 4 | 8,8,6,6 |

### Day 3

| exercise | sets | reps |
| --- | --- | --- |
| barbell triceps curls | 5 | 12,10,8,6,2 |
| close-grip barbell bench press | 5 | 12,10,8,6,2 |
| hammer curls | 4 | 12,10,8,6 |
| preacher curls | 4 | 12,10,8,6 |

## Weeks 3 and 4

### Day 1

| exercise | sets | reps |
| --- | --- | --- |
| barbell bench press | 5 | 8,6,4,2,1 |
| incline barbell bench press | 5 | 8,6,4,2,1 |
| close-grip lat pull downs | 4 | 8,8,8,8 |
| T-bar rows | 4 | 8,8,8,8 |

### Day 2

| exercise | sets | reps |
| --- | --- | --- |
| squats | 5 | 10,8,6,4,2 |
| dead lift | 5 | 10,8,6,4,2 |
| barbell military press | 5 | 8,6,4,2,1 |
| standing flyes | 4 | 8,8,6,6 |

### Day 3

| exercise | sets | reps |
| --- | --- | --- |
| barbell triceps curls | 5 | 12,10,8,6,2 |
| triceps push downs | 5 | 12,10,8,6,2 |
| reverse barbell curls | 4 | 12,10,8,6 |
| barbell curls | 4 | 12,10,8,6 |

# Strength Training
Three-Day Split four days a week
Synergistic Training

## Weeks 1 and 2

### Day 1

| exercise | sets | reps |
|---|---|---|
| barbell bench press | 5 | 8,6,4,2,1 |
| incline barbell bench press | 5 | 8,6,4,2,1 |
| close-grip barbell bench press | 5 | 8,6,4,2,1 |
| triceps push downs | 4 | 12,10,8,6 |

### Day 2

| exercise | sets | reps |
|---|---|---|
| wide-grip lat pull downs | 4 | 8,8,8,8 |
| hammer curls | 4 | 12,10,8,6 |
| preacher curls | 4 | 12,10,8,6 |
| bent-over barbell rows | 4 | 8,8,8,8 |

### Day 3

| exercise | sets | reps |
|---|---|---|
| squats | 5 | 10,8,6,4,2 |
| leg press | 5 | 10,8,6,4,2 |
| barbell military press | 5 | 8,6,4,2,1 |
| upright rows | 4 | 8,8,6,6 |

## Weeks 3 and 4

### Day 1

| exercise | sets | reps |
|---|---|---|
| incline barbell bench press | 5 | 8,6,4,2,1 |
| barbell triceps curls | 4 | 12,10,8,6 |
| flyes | 4 | 8,8,6,6 |
| skull crushers | 4 | 12,10,8,6 |

### Day 2

| exercise | sets | reps |
|---|---|---|
| close-grip lat pull downs | 4 | 8,8,8,8 |
| reverse barbell curls | 4 | 12,10,8,6 |
| T bar rows | 4 | 8,8,8,8 |
| concentration curls | 4 | 12,10,8,6 |

### Day 3

| exercise | sets | reps |
|---|---|---|
| squats | 5 | 10,8,6,4,2 |
| barbell military press | 5 | 8,6,4,2,1 |
| standing flyes | 4 | 8,8,6,6 |
| dead lift | 5 | 10,8,6,4,2 |

Program Level II

# Strength Training
Entire body every training day
Rest every other day

## Weeks 1 and 2

### Day 1

| exercise | sets | reps |
|---|---|---|
| barbell bench press | 5 | 8,6,4,2,1 |
| barbell military press | 5 | 8,6,4,2,1 |
| wide-grip lat pull downs | 4 | 8,8,8,8 |
| squats | 5 | 10,8,6,4,2 |
| incline barbell bench press | 4 | 8,6,4,2 |
| lunges | 4 | 10,8,8,6 |

### Day 2

| exercise | sets | reps |
|---|---|---|
| incline barbell bench press | 5 | 8,6,4,2,1 |
| barbell military press | 5 | 8,6,4,2,1 |
| close-grip lat pull downs | 4 | 8,8,8,8 |
| leg press | 5 | 10,8,6,4,2 |
| barbell bench press | 4 | 8,6,4,2 |
| dead lift | 5 | 10,8,6,4,2 |

### Day 3

| exercise | sets | reps |
|---|---|---|
| barbell bench press | 5 | 8,6,4,2,1 |
| barbell military press | 5 | 8,6,4,2,1 |
| wide-grip lat pull downs | 4 | 8,8,8,8 |
| squats | 5 | 10,8,6,4,2 |
| incline dumbbell bench press | 4 | 8,6,4,2 |
| lunges | 4 | 10,8,8,6 |

## Weeks 3 and 4

### Day 1

| exercise | sets | reps |
|---|---|---|
| barbell bench press | 5 | 8,6,4,2,1 |
| barbell military press | 5 | 8,6,4,2,1 |
| T-bar rows | 4 | 8,8,8,8 |
| leg press | 5 | 10,8,6,4,2 |
| incline barbell bench press | 4 | 8,6,4,2 |
| dead lift | 5 | 10,8,6,4,2 |

### Day 2

| exercise | sets | reps |
|---|---|---|
| incline barbell bench press | 5 | 8,6,4,2,1 |
| barbell military press | 5 | 8,6,4,2,1 |
| seated cable rows | 4 | 8,8,8,8 |
| squats | 5 | 10,8,6,4,2 |
| incline flyes | 4 | 8,6,4,2 |
| lunges | 5 | 10,8,6,4,2 |

### Day 3

| exercise | sets | reps |
|---|---|---|
| barbell bench press | 5 | 8,6,4,2,1 |
| barbell military press | 5 | 8,6,4,2,1 |
| bent-over barbell rows | 4 | 8,8,8,8 |
| leg press | 5 | 10,8,6,4,2 |
| incline barbell bench press | 4 | 8,6,4,2 |
| dead lift | 5 | 10,8,6,4,2 |

## Program Level III
# Strength Training
Three-Day Split four days a week -- Antagonistic Training

## Weeks 1 and 2

### Day 1

| exercise | sets | reps |
|---|---|---|
| barbell bench press | 5 | 8,6,4,2,1 |
| incline barbell bench press | 5 | 8,6,4,2,1 |
| wide-grip lat pull downs | 4 | 8,8,8,8 |
| seated cable rows | 4 | 8,8,8,8 |
| cable crossovers | 4 | 8,8,6,6 |
| bent-over barbell rows | 4 | 8,8,8,8 |

### Day 2

| exercise | sets | reps |
|---|---|---|
| squats | 5 | 10,8,6,4,2 |
| leg press | 5 | 10,8,6,4,2 |
| barbell military press | 5 | 8,6,4,2,1 |
| upright rows | 4 | 8,8,6,6 |
| lunges | 4 | 10,8,8,6 |
| barbell shrugs | 4 | 10,8,8,6 |

### Day 3

| exercise | sets | reps |
|---|---|---|
| barbell triceps curls | 5 | 12,10,8,6,2 |
| close-grip barbell bench press | 5 | 12,10,8,6,2 |
| hammer curls | 4 | 12,10,8,6 |
| preacher curls | 4 | 12,10,8,6 |
| bench dips | 5 | 12,10,8,6,2 |
| barbell curls | 4 | 12,10,8,6 |

## Weeks 3 and 4

### Day 1

| exercise | sets | reps |
|---|---|---|
| barbell bench press | 5 | 8,6,4,2,1 |
| incline barbell bench press | 5 | 8,6,4,2,1 |
| close-grip lat pull downs | 4 | 8,8,8,8 |
| T-bar rows | 4 | 8,8,8,8 |
| flyes | 4 | 10,8,8,6 |
| behind the neck pull downs | 4 | 8,8,8,8 |

### Day 2

| exercise | sets | reps |
|---|---|---|
| squats | 5 | 10,8,6,4,2 |
| dead lift | 5 | 10,8,6,4,2 |
| barbell military press | 5 | 8,6,4,2,1 |
| standing flyes | 4 | 8,8,6,6 |
| lunges | 4 | 10,8,8,6 |
| barbell shrugs | 4 | 10,8,8,6 |

### Day 3

| exercise | sets | reps |
|---|---|---|
| barbell triceps curls | 5 | 12,10,8,6,2 |
| triceps push downs | 5 | 12,10,8,6,2 |
| reverse barbell curls | 4 | 12,10,8,6 |
| barbell curls | 4 | 12,10,8,6 |
| dips | 5 | 12,10,8,6,2 |
| preacher curls | 4 | 12,10,8,6 |

## Program Level III
# Strength Training
Three-Day Split four days a week -- Synergistic Training

## Weeks 1 and 2

### Day 1

| exercise | sets | reps |
|---|---|---|
| barbell bench press | 5 | 8,6,4,2,1 |
| incline barbell bench press | 5 | 8,6,4,2,1 |
| close-grip barbell bench press | 5 | 8,6,4,2,1 |
| triceps push downs | 4 | 12,10,8,6 |
| flyes | 4 | 10,8,8,6 |
| skull crushers | 5 | 12,10,8,6,2 |

### Day 2

| exercise | sets | reps |
|---|---|---|
| wide-grip lat pull downs | 4 | 8,8,8,8 |
| hammer curls | 4 | 12,10,8,6 |
| preacher curls | 4 | 12,10,8,6 |
| bent-over barbell rows | 4 | 8,8,8,8 |
| seated cable rows | 4 | 8,8,8,8 |
| barbell curls | 4 | 12,10,8,6 |

### Day 3

| exercise | sets | reps |
|---|---|---|
| squats | 5 | 10,8,6,4,2 |
| leg press | 5 | 10,8,6,4,2 |
| barbell military press | 5 | 8,6,4,2,1 |
| upright rows | 4 | 8,8,6,6 |
| lunges | 4 | 10,8,8,6 |
| standing flyes | 4 | 8,8,6,6 |

## Weeks 3 and 4

### Day 1

| exercise | sets | reps |
|---|---|---|
| barbell bench press | 5 | 8,6,4,2,1 |
| incline barbell bench press | 5 | 8,6,4,2,1 |
| triceps kickbacks | 5 | 8,6,4,2,1 |
| triceps pull downs | 4 | 12,10,8,6 |
| incline flyes | 4 | 10,8,8,6 |
| barbell triceps curls | 5 | 12,10,8,6,2 |

### Day 2

| exercise | sets | reps |
|---|---|---|
| close-grip lat pull downs | 4 | 8,8,8,8 |
| reverse barbell curls | 4 | 12,10,8,6 |
| incline dumbbell curls | 4 | 12,10,8,6 |
| behind the neck pull downs | 4 | 8,8,8,8 |
| T-bar rows | 4 | 8,8,8,8 |
| concentration curls | 4 | 12,10,8,6 |

### Day 3

| exercise | sets | reps |
|---|---|---|
| squats | 5 | 10,8,6,4,2 |
| dead lift | 5 | 10,8,6,4,2 |
| barbell military press | 5 | 8,6,4,2,1 |
| lateral raises | 4 | 8,8,8,8 |
| leg curls | 4 | 10,8,8,6 |
| upright rows | 4 | 8,8,6,6 |

## Program Level III
# Strength Training
Two-Day Split 4 days per week
Upper & lower body training on the same day -- Antagonistic Training

## Weeks 1 and 2

### Days 1 and 3

| exercise | sets | reps |
|---|---|---|
| barbell bench press | 5 | 8,6,4,2,1 |
| wide-grip lat pull downs | 4 | 8,8,8,8 |
| barbell military press | 5 | 8,6,4,2,1 |
| leg curls | 5 | 10,8,6,4,2 |

### Days 2 and 4

| exercise | sets | reps |
|---|---|---|
| squats | 5 | 10,8,6,4,2 |
| leg press | 5 | 10,8,6,4,2 |
| barbell curls | 4 | 12,10,8,6 |
| skull crushers | 5 | 12,10,8,6,2 |

## Weeks 3 and 4

### Days 1 and 3

| exercise | sets | reps |
|---|---|---|
| barbell bench press | 5 | 8,6,4,2,1 |
| close-grip lat pull downs | 4 | 8,8,8,8 |
| barbell military press | 5 | 8,6,4,2,1 |
| leg curls | 5 | 10,8,6,4,2 |

### Days 2 and 4

| exercise | sets | reps |
|---|---|---|
| squats | 5 | 10,8,6,4,2 |
| dead lift | 5 | 10,8,6,4,2 |
| preacher curls | 4 | 12,10,8,6 |
| triceps push downs | 4 | 12,10,8,6 |

## Program Level III
# Strength Training
Two-Day Split 4 days per week
Upper & lower body training on different days

## Weeks 1 and 2

### Days 1 and 3

| exercise | sets | reps |
|---|---|---|
| barbell bench press | 5 | 8,6,4,2,1 |
| wide-grip lat pull downs | 4 | 8,8,8,8 |
| barbell military press | 5 | 8,6,4,2,1 |
| hammer curls | 4 | 12,10,8,6 |

### Days 2 and 4

| exercise | sets | reps |
|---|---|---|
| squats | 5 | 10,8,6,4,2 |
| leg press | 5 | 10,8,6,4,2 |
| lunges | 5 | 10,8,6,4,2 |
| standing calf raises | 4 | 20,20,20,20 |

## Weeks 3 and 4

### Days 1 and 3

| exercise | sets | reps |
|---|---|---|
| barbell bench press | 5 | 8,6,4,2,1 |
| close-grip lat pull downs | 4 | 8,8,8,8 |
| barbell military press | 5 | 8,6,4,2,1 |
| reverse curls | 4 | 12,10,8,6 |

### Days 2 and 4

| exercise | sets | reps |
|---|---|---|
| leg press | 5 | 10,8,6,4,2 |
| Leg extensions | 5 | 10,8,6,4,2 |
| squats | 5 | 10,8,6,4,2 |
| seated calf raises | 4 | 20,20,20,20 |

# Strength Training
Two-Day Split 4 days per week
Upper & lower body training on the same day -- Synergistic Training

## Weeks 1 and 2

### Days 1 and 3

| exercise | sets | reps |
|---|---|---|
| barbell bench press | 5 | 8,6,4,2,1 |
| upright rows | 5 | 8,6,4,2,1 |
| incline barbell bench press | 5 | 8,6,4,2,1 |
| leg curls | 5 | 10,8,6,4,2 |

### Days 2 and 4

| exercise | sets | reps |
|---|---|---|
| wide-grip lat pull downs | 4 | 8,8,8,8 |
| hammer curls | 4 | 12,10,8,6 |
| squats | 5 | 10,8,6,4,2 |
| leg extensions | 4 | 8,8,6,6 |

## Weeks 3 and 4

### Days 1 and 3

| exercise | sets | reps |
|---|---|---|
| barbell bench press | 5 | 8,6,4,2,1 |
| upright rows | 5 | 8,6,4,2,1 |
| incline barbell bench press | 5 | 8,6,4,2,1 |
| leg curls | 5 | 10,8,6,4,2 |

### Days 2 and 4

| exercise | sets | reps |
|---|---|---|
| close-grip lat pull downs | 4 | 8,8,8,8 |
| reverse curls | 4 | 12,10,8,6 |
| leg press | 5 | 10,8,6,4,2 |
| leg extensions | 4 | 8,8,6,6 |

# Strength Training
Entire body every training day -- Rest every other day

## Weeks 1 and 2

### Day 1

| exercise | sets | reps |
|---|---|---|
| barbell bench press | 5 | 8,6,4,2,1 |
| barbell military press | 5 | 8,6,4,2,1 |
| wide-grip lat pull downs | 4 | 8,8,8,8 |
| squats | 5 | 10,8,6,4,2 |
| incline barbell bench press | 4 | 8,6,4,2 |
| lunges | 4 | 10,8,8,6 |
| bent-over barbell rows | 4 | 8,8,8,8 |
| incline flyes | 4 | 8,8,6,6 |

### Day 2

| exercise | sets | reps |
|---|---|---|
| incline barbell bench press | 5 | 8,6,4,2,1 |
| barbell military press | 5 | 8,6,4,2,1 |
| close-grip lat pull downs | 4 | 8,8,8,8 |
| leg press | 5 | 10,8,6,4,2 |
| barbell bench press | 4 | 8,6,4,2 |
| dead lift | 5 | 10,8,6,4,2 |
| seated cable rows | 4 | 8,8,8,8 |
| flyes | 4 | 8,8,6,6 |

### Day 3

| exercise | sets | reps |
|---|---|---|
| barbell bench press | 5 | 8,6,4,2,1 |
| barbell military press | 5 | 8,6,4,2,1 |
| wide-grip lat pull downs | 4 | 8,8,8,8 |
| squats | 5 | 10,8,6,4,2 |
| incline barbell bench press | 4 | 8,6,4,2 |
| lunges | 4 | 10,8,8,6 |
| bent-over barbell rows | 4 | 8,8,8,8 |
| incline flyes | 4 | 8,8,6,6 |

## Weeks 3 and 4

### Day 1

| exercise | sets | reps |
|---|---|---|
| barbell bench press | 5 | 8,6,4,2,1 |
| barbell military press | 5 | 8,6,4,2,1 |
| T-bar rows | 4 | 8,8,8,8 |
| leg press | 5 | 10,8,6,4,2 |
| incline barbell bench press | 4 | 8,6,4,2 |
| dead lift | 5 | 10,8,6,4,2 |
| wide-grip lat pull downs | 4 | 8,8,8,8 |
| cable crossovers | 4 | 8,8,6,6 |

### Day 2

| exercise | sets | reps |
|---|---|---|
| incline barbell bench press | 5 | 8,6,4,2,1 |
| barbell military press | 5 | 8,6,4,2,1 |
| seated cable rows | 4 | 8,8,8,8 |
| squats | 5 | 10,8,6,4,2 |
| incline flyes | 4 | 8,6,4,2 |
| lunges | 5 | 10,8,6,4,2 |
| close-grip lat pull downs | 4 | 8,8,8,8 |
| barbell bench press | 4 | 8,8,6,6 |

### Day 3

| exercise | sets | reps |
|---|---|---|
| barbell bench press | 5 | 8,6,4,2,1 |
| barbell military press | 5 | 8,6,4,2,1 |
| bent-over barbell rows | 4 | 8,8,8,8 |
| leg press | 5 | 10,8,6,4,2 |
| incline barbell bench press | 4 | 8,6,4,2 |
| dead lift | 5 | 10,8,6,4,2 |
| wide-grip lat pull downs | 4 | 8,8,8,8 |
| cable crossovers | 4 | 8,8,6,6 |

## Program Level IV
# Strength Training
Two-Day Split 4 days per week
Upper & lower body training on different days

## Weeks 1 and 2

### Days 1 and 3

| exercise | sets | reps |
|---|---|---|
| barbell bench press | 5 | 8,6,4,2,1 |
| wide-grip lat pull downs | 4 | 8,8,8,8 |
| barbell military press | 5 | 8,6,4,2,1 |
| hammer curls | 4 | 12,10,8,6 |
| close-grip barbell bench press | 4 | 10,10,8,8 |
| bent-over barbell rows | 4 | 8,8,8,8 |

### Days 2 and 4

| exercise | sets | reps |
|---|---|---|
| squats | 5 | 10,8,6,4,2 |
| leg press | 5 | 10,8,6,4,2 |
| leg curls | 4 | 8,8,6,6 |
| lunges | 4 | 10,8,8,6 |
| leg extensions | 4 | 8,8,6,6 |
| standing calf raises | 4 | 20,20,20,20 |

## Weeks 3 and 4

### Days 1 and 3

| exercise | sets | reps |
|---|---|---|
| barbell bench press | 5 | 8,6,4,2,1 |
| close-grip lat pull downs | 4 | 8,8,8,8 |
| barbell military press | 5 | 8,6,4,2,1 |
| reverse curls | 4 | 12,10,8,6 |
| incline barbell bench press | 4 | 10,10,8,8 |
| T-bar rows | 4 | 0,0,0,0 |

### Days 2 and 4

| exercise | sets | reps |
|---|---|---|
| leg press | 5 | 10,8,6,4,2 |
| squats | 5 | 10,8,6,4,2 |
| lunges | 4 | 10,8,6,4,2 |
| leg extensions | 4 | 10,8,8,6 |
| leg curls | 4 | 8,8,6,6 |
| standing calf raises | 4 | 20,20,20,20 |

## Program Level IV
# Strength Training
Three-Day Split four days a week -- Antagonistic Training

## Weeks 1 and 2

### Day 1

| exercise | sets | reps |
|---|---|---|
| barbell bench press | 5 | 8,6,4,2,1 |
| incline barbell bench press | 5 | 8,6,4,2,1 |
| wide-grip lat pull downs | 4 | 8,8,8,8 |
| seated cable rows | 4 | 8,8,8,8 |
| cable crossovers | 4 | 8,8,6,6 |
| bent-over barbell rows | 4 | 8,8,8,8 |
| incline flyes | 4 | 10,8,6,6 |
| T-bar rows | 4 | 8,8,8,8 |

### Day 2

| exercise | sets | reps |
|---|---|---|
| squats | 5 | 10,8,6,4,2 |
| leg press | 5 | 10,8,6,4,2 |
| barbell military press | 5 | 8,6,4,2,1 |
| upright rows | 4 | 8,8,6,6 |
| lunges | 4 | 10,8,8,6 |
| barbell shrugs | 4 | 10,8,8,6 |
| dead lift | 5 | 10,8,6,4,2 |
| bent-over lateral raises | 4 | 10,8,8,6 |

### Day 3

| exercise | sets | reps |
|---|---|---|
| barbell triceps curls | 5 | 12,10,8,6,2 |
| close-grip barbell bench press | 5 | 12,10,8,6,2 |
| hammer curls | 4 | 12,10,8,6 |
| preacher curls | 4 | 12,10,8,6 |
| bench dips | 5 | 12,10,8,6,2 |
| barbell curls | 4 | 12,10,8,6 |
| skull crushers | 5 | 12,10,8,6,2 |
| concentration curls | 4 | 12,10,8,6 |

## Weeks 3 and 4

### Day 1

| exercise | sets | reps |
|---|---|---|
| barbell bench press | 5 | 8,6,4,2,1 |
| incline barbell bench press | 5 | 8,6,4,2,1 |
| close-grip lat pull downs | 4 | 8,8,8,8 |
| T-bar rows | 4 | 8,8,8,8 |
| flyes | 4 | 10,8,8,6 |
| behind the neck pull downs | 4 | 8,8,8,8 |
| cable crossovers | 4 | 10,8,8,6 |
| bent-over barbell rows | 4 | 8,8,8,8 |

### Day 2

| exercise | sets | reps |
|---|---|---|
| squats | 5 | 10,8,6,4,2 |
| dead lift | 5 | 10,8,6,4,2 |
| barbell military press | 5 | 8,6,4,2,1 |
| standing flyes | 4 | 8,8,6,6 |
| lunges | 4 | 10,8,8,6 |
| barbell shrugs | 4 | 10,8,8,6 |
| leg press | 5 | 10,8,6,4,2 |
| upright rows | 4 | 8,8,6,6 |

### Day 3

| exercise | sets | reps |
|---|---|---|
| barbell triceps curls | 5 | 12,10,8,6,2 |
| triceps push downs | 5 | 12,10,8,6,2 |
| reverse barbell curls | 4 | 12,10,8,6 |
| barbell curls | 4 | 12,10,8,6 |
| dips | 5 | 12,10,8,6,2 |
| preacher curls | 4 | 12,10,8,6 |
| skull crushers | 5 | 12,10,8,6,2 |
| incline dumbbell curls | 4 | 12,10,8,6 |

## Program Level IV
# Strength Training
Three-Day Split four days a week -- Synergistic Training
## Weeks 1 and 2

### Day 1

| exercise | sets | reps |
|---|---|---|
| barbell bench press | 5 | 8,6,4,2,1 |
| incline barbell bench press | 5 | 8,6,4,2,1 |
| close-grip barbell bench press | 5 | 8,6,4,2,1 |
| triceps push downs | 4 | 12,10,8,6 |
| flyes | 4 | 10,8,8,6 |
| skull crushers | 5 | 12,10,8,6,2 |
| dips | 4 | 8,8,8,8 |
| barbell triceps curls | 5 | 12,10,8,6,2 |

### Day 2

| exercise | sets | reps |
|---|---|---|
| wide-grip lat pull downs | 4 | 8,8,8,8 |
| hammer curls | 4 | 12,10,8,6 |
| preacher curls | 4 | 12,10,8,6 |
| bent-over barbell rows | 4 | 8,8,8,8 |
| seated cable rows | 4 | 8,8,8,8 |
| barbell curls | 4 | 12,10,8,6 |
| incline dumbbell curls | 4 | 12,10,8,6 |
| T-bar rows | 4 | 8,8,8,8 |

### Day 3

| exercise | sets | reps |
|---|---|---|
| squats | 5 | 10,8,6,4,2 |
| leg press | 5 | 10,8,6,4,2 |
| barbell military press | 5 | 8,6,4,2,1 |
| upright rows | 4 | 8,8,6,6 |
| lunges | 4 | 10,8,8,6 |
| standing flyes | 4 | 8,8,6,6 |
| leg extensions | 4 | 8,8,6,6 |
| lateral raises | 4 | 8,8,8,8 |

## Weeks 3 and 4

### Day 1

| exercise | sets | reps |
|---|---|---|
| barbell bench press | 5 | 8,6,4,2,1 |
| incline barbell bench press | 5 | 8,6,4,2,1 |
| dumbbell triceps curls | 4 | 8,6,6,6 |
| triceps pull downs | 4 | 12,10,8,6 |
| incline flyes | 4 | 10,8,8,6 |
| one-arm triceps extensions | 5 | 12,10,8,6,2 |
| bench dips | 4 | 8,8,8,8 |
| triceps kickbacks | 4 | 8,8,8,8 |

### Day 2

| exercise | sets | reps |
|---|---|---|
| close-grip lat pull downs | 4 | 8,8,8,8 |
| reverse barbell curls | 4 | 12,10,8,6 |
| concentration curls | 4 | 12,10,8,6 |
| behind the neck pull downs | 4 | 8,8,8,8 |
| seated cable rows | 4 | 8,8,8,8 |
| barbell curls | 4 | 12,10,8,6 |
| dumbbell curls | 4 | 12,10,8,6 |
| one-arm dumbbell rows | 4 | 8,8,8,8 |

### Day 3

| exercise | sets | reps |
|---|---|---|
| squats | 5 | 10,8,6,4,2 |
| dead lift | 5 | 10,8,6,4,2 |
| barbell military press | 5 | 8,6,4,2,1 |
| upright rows | 4 | 8,8,6,6 |
| leg curls | 4 | 10,8,8,6 |
| standing flyes | 4 | 8,8,6,6 |
| standing calf raises | 4 | 20,20,20,20 |
| front raises | 4 | 8,8,8,8 |

## Program Level IV
# Strength Training
Two-Day Split 4 days per week -- Upper & lower body training on the same day -- Antagonistic Training
## Weeks 1 and 2

### Days 1 and 3

| exercise | sets | reps |
|---|---|---|
| barbell bench press | 5 | 8,6,4,2,1 |
| wide-grip lat pull downs | 4 | 8,8,8,8 |
| incline barbell bench press | 5 | 8,6,4,2,1 |
| barbell military press | 5 | 10,8,6,4,2 |
| leg curls | 5 | 8,6,4,2,1 |
| standing calf raises | 4 | 20,20,20,20 |

### Days 2 and 4

| exercise | sets | reps |
|---|---|---|
| squats | 5 | 10,8,6,4,2 |
| leg press | 5 | 10,8,6,4,2 |
| barbell curls | 4 | 12,10,8,6 |
| skull crushers | 5 | 12,10,8,6,2 |
| hammer curls | 4 | 12,10,8,6 |
| barbell triceps curls | 4 | 12,10,8,6 |

## Weeks 3 and 4

### Days 1 and 3

| exercise | sets | reps |
|---|---|---|
| barbell bench press | 5 | 8,6,4,2,1 |
| close-grip lat pull downs | 4 | 8,8,8,8 |
| barbell military press | 5 | 8,6,4,2,1 |
| leg curls | 5 | 10,8,6,4,2 |
| good mornings | 4 | 15,15,15,15 |
| incline barbell bench press | 5 | 8,6,4,2,1 |

### Days 2 and 4

| exercise | sets | reps |
|---|---|---|
| squats | 5 | 10,8,6,4,2 |
| dead lift | 5 | 10,8,6,4,2 |
| preacher curls | 4 | 12,10,8,6 |
| triceps push downs | 4 | 12,10,8,6 |
| reverse curls | 4 | 12,10,8,6 |
| triceps kickbacks | 4 | 12,10,8,6 |

### Program Level IV
# Strength Training
Two-Day Split 4 days per week

Upper & lower body training on the same day
Synergistic Training

## Weeks 1 and 2

### Days 1 and 3

| exercise | sets | reps |
|---|---|---|
| barbell bench press | 5 | 8,6,4,2,1 |
| barbell military press | 5 | 8,6,4,2,1 |
| incline barbell bench press | 5 | 8,6,4,2,1 |
| leg curls | 5 | 10,8,6,4,2 |
| close grip barbell bench press | 4 | 10,10,8,8 |
| good mornings | 4 | 15,15,15,15 |

### Days 2 and 4

| exercise | sets | reps |
|---|---|---|
| wide-grip lat pull downs | 4 | 8,8,8,8 |
| hammer curls | 4 | 12,10,8,6 |
| squats | 5 | 10,8,6,4,2 |
| leg extensions | 4 | 8,8,6,6 |
| bent-over rows | 4 | 8,8,8,8 |
| lunges | 4 | 10,8,8,6 |

## Weeks 3 and 4

### Days 1 and 3

| exercise | sets | reps |
|---|---|---|
| barbell bench press | 5 | 8,6,4,2,1 |
| barbell military press | 5 | 8,6,4,2,1 |
| incline barbell bench press | 5 | 8,6,4,2,1 |
| leg curls | 5 | 10,8,6,4,2 |
| barbell triceps curls | 4 | 10,10,8,8 |
| standing calf raises | 4 | 20,20,20,20 |

### Days 2 and 4

| exercise | sets | reps |
|---|---|---|
| close-grip lat pull downs | 4 | 8,8,8,8 |
| reverse curls | 4 | 12,10,8,6 |
| leg press | 5 | 10,8,6,4,2 |
| leg extensions | 4 | 8,8,6,6 |
| bent-over barbell rows | 4 | 8,8,8,8 |
| dead lift | 5 | 10,8,6,4,2 |

## Program Level V
# Strength Training
Two-Day Split 4 days per week

Upper & lower body training on the same day
Antagonistic Training

## Weeks 1 and 2

### Days 1 and 3

| exercise | sets | reps |
|---|---|---|
| barbell bench press | 5 | 8,6,4,2,1 |
| wide-grip lat pull downs | 4 | 8,8,8,8 |
| barbell military press | 5 | 8,6,4,2,1 |
| leg curls | 5 | 10,8,6,4,2 |
| incline barbell bench press | 5 | 8,6,4,2,1 |
| standing calf raises | 4 | 20,20,20,20 |
| T-bar rows | 4 | 8,8,8,8 |
| standing flyes | 4 | 8,8,6,6 |

### Days 2 and 4

| exercise | sets | reps |
|---|---|---|
| squats | 5 | 10,8,6,4,2 |
| leg press | 5 | 10,8,6,4,2 |
| barbell curls | 4 | 12,10,8,6 |
| skull crushers | 5 | 12,10,8,6,2 |
| hammer curls | 4 | 12,10,8,6 |
| barbell triceps curls | 4 | 12,10,8,6 |
| lunges | 4 | 10,8,8,6 |
| triceps push downs | 4 | 12,10,8,6 |

## Weeks 3 and 4

### Days 1 and 3

| exercise | sets | reps |
|---|---|---|
| barbell bench press | 5 | 8,6,4,2,1 |
| close-grip lat pull downs | 4 | 8,8,8,8 |
| barbell military press | 5 | 8,6,4,2,1 |
| leg curls | 5 | 10,8,6,4,2 |
| good mornings | 4 | 15,15,15,15 |
| incline barbell bench press | 5 | 8,6,4,2,1 |
| seated cable rows | 4 | 8,8,8,8 |
| upright rows | 4 | 8,8,6,6 |

### Days 2 and 4

| exercise | sets | reps |
|---|---|---|
| squats | 5 | 10,8,6,4,2 |
| dead lift | 5 | 10,8,6,4,2 |
| preacher curls | 4 | 12,10,8,6 |
| triceps push downs | 4 | 12,10,8,6 |
| reverse curls | 4 | 12,10,8,6 |
| barbell triceps curls | 4 | 12,10,8,6 |
| standing calf raises | 4 | 20,20,20,20 |
| bench dips | 3 | 15,15,15 |

**166**

## Program Level V
# Strength Training
Two-Day Split 4 days per week
Upper & lower body training on different days

## Weeks 1 and 2

### Days 1 and 3

| exercise | sets | reps |
|---|---|---|
| barbell bench press | 5 | 8,6,4,2,1 |
| wide-grip lat pull downs | 4 | 8,8,8,8 |
| barbell military press | 5 | 8,6,4,2,1 |
| hammer curls | 4 | 12,10,8,6 |
| close-grip barbell bench press | 4 | 10,10,8,8 |
| bent-over barbell rows | 4 | 8,8,8,8 |
| incline barbell bench press | 5 | 8,6,4,2,1 |
| skull crushers | 5 | 12,10,8,6,2 |

### Days 2 and 4

| exercise | sets | reps |
|---|---|---|
| squats | 5 | 10,8,6,4,2 |
| leg press | 5 | 10,8,6,4,2 |
| standing calf raises | 4 | 20,20,20,20 |
| lunges | 4 | 10,8,8,6 |
| leg extensions | 4 | 8,8,6,6 |
| leg curls | 4 | 8,8,6,6 |
| dead lift | 4 | 8,6,4,2 |
| seated calf raises | 4 | 20,20,20,20 |

## Weeks 3 and 4

### Days 1 and 3

| exercise | sets | reps |
|---|---|---|
| barbell bench press | 5 | 8,6,4,2,1 |
| close-grip lat pull downs | 4 | 8,8,8,8 |
| barbell military press | 5 | 8,6,4,2,1 |
| reverse curls | 4 | 12,10,8,6 |
| incline barbell bench press | 4 | 10,10,8,8 |
| T-bar rows | 4 | 8,8,8,8 |
| barbell triceps curls | 5 | 12,10,8,6,2 |
| barbell curls | 5 | 12,10,8,6,2 |

### Days 2 and 4

| exercise | sets | reps |
|---|---|---|
| leg press | 5 | 10,8,6,4,2 |
| squats | 5 | 10,8,6,4,2 |
| lunges | 4 | 10,8,6,4,2 |
| dead lift | 4 | 10,8,8,6 |
| leg curls | 4 | 8,8,6,6 |
| leg extensions | 4 | 8,8,6,6 |
| standing calf raises | 4 | 8,6,4,2 |
| seated calf raises | 4 | 20,20,20,20 |

# Strength Training
Two-Day Split 4 days per week
Upper & lower body training on the same day
Synergistic Training

## Weeks 1 and 2

### Days 1 and 3

| exercise | sets | reps |
|---|---|---|
| barbell bench press | 5 | 8,6,4,2,1 |
| barbell military press | 5 | 8,6,4,2,1 |
| incline barbell bench press | 5 | 8,6,4,2,1 |
| leg curls | 5 | 10,8,6,4,2 |
| close-grip barbell bench press | 4 | 10,10,8,8 |
| good mornings | 4 | 15,15,15,15 |
| skull crushers | 5 | 12,10,8,6,2 |
| upright rows | 4 | 8,8,6,6 |

### Days 2 and 4

| exercise | sets | reps |
|---|---|---|
| wide-grip lat pull downs | 4 | 8,8,8,8 |
| hammer curls | 4 | 12,10,8,6 |
| squats | 5 | 10,8,6,4,2 |
| leg extensions | 4 | 8,8,6,6 |
| bent-over barbell rows | 4 | 8,8,8,8 |
| lunges | 4 | 10,8,8,6 |
| T-bar rows | 4 | 8,8,8,8 |
| preacher curls | 4 | 12,10,8,6 |

## Weeks 3 and 4

### Days 1 and 3

| exercise | sets | reps |
|---|---|---|
| barbell bench press | 5 | 8,6,4,2,1 |
| barbell military press | 5 | 8,6,4,2,1 |
| incline barbell bench press | 5 | 8,6,4,2,1 |
| leg curls | 5 | 10,8,6,4,2 |
| barbell triceps curls | 4 | 10,10,8,8 |
| standing calf raises | 4 | 20,20,20,20 |
| triceps pull downs | 4 | 12,10,8,6 |
| standing flyes | 4 | 8,8,6,6 |

### Days 2 and 4

| exercise | sets | reps |
|---|---|---|
| close-grip lat pull downs | 4 | 8,8,8,8 |
| reverse curls | 4 | 12,10,8,6 |
| leg press | 5 | 10,8,6,4,2 |
| leg extensions | 4 | 8,8,6,6 |
| bent-over barbell rows | 4 | 8,8,8,8 |
| dead lift | 5 | 10,8,6,4,2 |
| seated cable rows | 4 | 8,8,8,8 |
| barbell curls | 4 | 12,10,8,6 |

# NOTES

# Do You Play Competitive Sports?

If you do play competitive sports, we have **FREE STUFF** for you!

Email **athletes@sportsworkout.com** and tell us what level you compete at and how this book has helped you!

- **Recreational**
- **High School**
- **College**
- **Semi Professional**
- **Professional**

Find out what sort of **FREE STUFF** we have for you!

**athletes@sportsworkout.com**

*sports*workout.com

# Members Only

*sports*workout.com

## SportsWorkout.com

introduces Ryan Lee's Sport-Specific membership, the world's largest strength & conditioning online membership site!

**Even the best in the business agree this membership is invaluable:**

*"Simply the best and most complete sports training resource I've ever used. If you are serious about improving your sports performance, I highly recommend joining today!"*

**Duane Carlisle**
**NFL** Philadelphia Eagles Speed Consultant

*"I was just introduced to your site by a colleague of mine and I wanted to let you know how impressed I was. I will certainly recommend that my athletes check out your site."*

**Matt Nichol**
**NHL** Toronto Maple Leafs Head Strength Coach

## 12 months of access to:

➤ Over 5,000 pages of sport-specific articles, programs, and training tips created by professional strength coaches

➤ FREE UNLIMITED Sports Training Consulting via email with a detailed response guaranteed within 48 hours ($900 monthly value!)

➤ Members Only discussion forum with some of the brightest minds in sports training

➤ New articles, programs, video clips, & exercise images added every week

➤ Audio interviews with professional strength coaches

## Bonus Items!

➤ The Ultimate Guide to Weight Training for Sports ($37 value!)

➤ The Sports Buddy ($29.95 value!)

➤ Strength Ball ($8.95 value!)

➤ Fitness Training e-Charts ($15 value!)

## Free Shipping & Handling!

If you order now, we'll pay all shipping costs, and have all bonus items delivered to your door, absolutely free!

**For a very limited time, if you subscribe to our e-Training program all of this will be yours COMPLETELY FREE!**

**Just go to** www.SportsWorkout.com/freemembership

Even if you cancel your e-Training subscription, you still get to keep this 12 month Membership free of charge! There are no contracts to sign and you can cancel at any time for any reason, no questions asked.

COMPLETELY FREE

Go to **www.SportsWorkout.com/freemembership** or call **1-866-S-WORKOUT (796-7568)** to Order!

# the
# *SportsBuddy*

To prepare the Sports Buddy, place the small piece at the bottom of the string through a plate (as pictured) so that you are able to securely use the Sports Buddy to lift the plate off the ground.

**Starting Position**

Hold the Sports Buddy out in front of your body with your arms extended and your hands at both ends using an overhand grip. For maximum results, grip the Sports Buddy with your index fingers and thumbs in the air not touching the Sports Buddy.

**Recommended weight to use with the Sports Buddy: 2.5 lbs**

If you don t want to travel to the gym every day to use the Sports Buddy, you can purchase weights at ANY sporting goods store for about $1.00 to $2.00 each.

## *sports*workout.com

## *General Instructions*

1 Slowly roll your wrists and hands backwards winding the weight up to the roller.

2 At this point, slowly lower the weight back to its original position by rolling your wrists and hands forward.

3 Next, continue with the same motion of rolling your wrists forward slowly, bringing the weight back up to the roller.

4 Finally, slowly lower the weight back to its original position by rolling your wrists and hands backwards and repeat.

If your main goal is to increase the strength in your dominant forearm and wrist, then wind the string to the same side as the arm you are trying to work. This will make the arm work harder when using the Sports Buddy.

# NOTES

# The Ultimate Guide to Weight Training for Sports Series

**The Ultimate Guide to Weight Training for Sports Series** is the most comprehensive and up-to-date sports-specific training series in the world today. Each book contains descriptions and photographs of over 80 of the most effective weight training, flexibility, and abdominal exercises used by athletes worldwide.

The reason books in this series are so popular is simple: While all of the books seem similar, each book features unique year-round sport-specific weight-training programs guaranteed to improve your performance and get you results.

No other sports books to date have been so well designed, so easy to use, and so committed to weight training. These books take you from the off-season to the in-season, and are loaded with dozens of tips and pointers to help you maximize your training and improve your performance.

Both beginners and advanced athletes and weight trainers can follow this book and utilize its programs. From recreational to professional, thousands of athletes all over the world are already benefiting from this book and its techniques, and now you can too!

The series has sold tens of thousands of copies to athletes all over the world including the LSU NCAA 2003 National Championship football team among countless professional and top collegiate athletes. Readers have enjoyed the interactive aspects of the books by being able to access hidden URLs for e-training charts and testing pages. Readers are also encouraged to submit questions to trainers for additional assistance.

# www.sportsworkout.com

*sports*workout.com

# Sport-Specific Online! Training
## One-on-One Training with the Author

Hi,

My name is Rob Price. If you enjoyed my book and would like to receive one-on-one online personal training from me for customized workout programs and 24/7 consultation, log onto www.SportsWorkout.com where you'll find more information and a free demo.

I've literally trained hundreds of athletes online over the past few years of all ages and skill levels, and have worked individually with each one of them to specifically tailor training regimens for their individual needs. My specialty is sport-specific training. I use cutting edge software to provide each of my clients with the ultimate online training experience.

As one of my clients, you'll have full access to me 24/7 and I'll be able to track all of your workouts. Spots are limited however, as I only train a small number of clients so I can give each one of them my fullest attention. This is not some impersonal plug and chug computer program. You get to work with me personally, one-on-one, and I get to help you achieve all of your athletic and personal goals.

The full price of this entire service comes to a fraction of the cost I charge my clients in person, and **if you use the following coupon code,**

## you'll get half off the first month!

### Coupon code  ADET12

There are no commitments and you can cancel any time.

Feel free to email me at
**etraining@SportsWorkout.com** if you have any questions and I will be happy to assist you in any way that I can.

I look forward to hearing from you!

Rob

***sports*workout.com**

## Testimonials

**February 23, 2006**

"I've been using your e-Training for Tennis service for the past month or so, and I must say, this program has remarkably improved my performance on the court. Fatigue has disappeared and the power and agility I now have while playing the game is incredible. **My one-handed-backhand that was once a weakness has become a blazing weapon.** Ground strokes are more powerful than ever and my serve just kills. I maintain the same amount of intensity at all times, start to finish thanks to the endurance training my trainer has me doing. This has resulted in numerous wins, and now, a national ranking. **I owe it all to you.** The programs were easy, simple and most important, efficient. I can't wait to get through the whole program to get to that holy peak performance period."
**Van A., Nationally Ranked Tennis Player**

**April 11, 2005**

"I've been a boxing trainer for 14 years and have trained many top notch fighters. You gave me a list of specific exercises for boxing that I never new existed. **My boxers are on average quicker, faster, and stronger than they have ever been before.** Not only that, but they are getting these benefits without struggling to maintain their weights. Personally, I use a lot of what you've taught me in my everyday life."
**Mike S., Boxing Trainer**

**February 22, 2006**

"I've been using the e-Training for Golf for 8 weeks. I must say the results are amazing. **I have added 7mph to my driver swing speed (109mph to 116mph) and my flexibility has increased dramatically.** I have played a few rounds and feel I control the club much better at the top. I also don't fatigue at the end of the round. I never really thought working out made much of a difference, but your program works. A few friends just subscribed and have started their own programs. Thanks for a great service!"
**Chuck S.**